OEDIPUS REX

(OEDIPUS THE KING)

By SOPHOCLES

Translated by E. H. PLUMPTRE

Introduction by JOHN W. WHITE

Oedipus Rex (Oedipus the King)
By Sophocles
Translated by Edward Hayes Plumptre
Introduction by John Williams White

Print ISBN 13: 978-1-4209-5346-6
eBook ISBN 13: 978-1-4209-5347-3

This edition copyright © 2016. Digireads.com Publishing.

Cover Image: A detail of "The Blind Oedipus Commending his Children to the Gods", by Bénigne Gagneraux, 1784. Oil on canvas.

Please visit *www.digireads.com*

CONTENTS

Introduction 5

Introductory Note 23

DRAMATIS PERSONAE 24

OEDIPUS REX 25

Introduction

ADAPTED FROM SCHNEIDEWIN.

Laïus son of Labdacus, king of Thebes, had been warned by an oracle of Apollo that he was destined to die by the hand of a son whom he should beget from his wife Jocasta, daughter of Menœceus. By what offence he had incurred this doom, Sophocles leaves untold; not so the pretended oracle:—

Λάϊε Λαβδακίδη, παίδων γένος ὅλβιον αἰτεῖς.

δώσω τοι φίλον υἱόν · ἀτὰρ πεπρωμένον ἐστὶν

σοῦ παιδὸς χείρεσσι λιπεῖν φάος · ὡς γὰρ ἔνευσεν

Ζεὺς Κρονίδης Πέλοπος στυγεραῖς ἀραῖσι πιθήσας,

οὖ φίλον ἥρπασας υἱόν · ὁ δ᾽ ηὔξατό σοι τάδε πάντα.

Accordingly, a son being born to him, Laïus binds his ankles together, and in this condition gives him into the hands of a slave, with orders to expose him upon the mountain. So Jocasta herself tells the story, 711 sqq., but suppresses some of the particulars. One of the omissions the old slave himself supplies, to the effect that he received the child, with command to make away with it, the rather from the mother's own hands, 1173, its feet being bound with a thong through holes cruelly bored in its ankles, which treatment was intended, without killing it outright, to insure its perishing, and to prevent its being taken up by others. Jocasta also keeps back the fact that it was on the subject of posterity that Laïus consulted Apollo, who warned him against begetting a son. Cf. 4184. The slave, however, takes compassion on the babe, and gives it, on Mount Cithaeron, to a herdsman from Corinth, 1142 sq. But he, instead of rearing it for himself, gives it to his childless master, King Polybus, and his wife Merope. With kindly affection the pair bring up the foundling, which, from its swelled feet, they name Oedipus (1036). He is generally accounted the first of the citizens of Corinth, until an apparently insignificant occurrence disturbs him in his youthful felicity. At a banquet,—as he himself, 779 sqq., relates,—one of his drunken companions assails him with the reproach that he is only the supposititious son of Polybus. Being stung by the affront, he with difficulty restrains himself for that day. On the morrow he presents himself before father and mother, tells them what has happened, and wishes to learn the truth. They are incensed against the author of the taunt, but fail to satisfy his doubts. The reproach still rankles in his breast, and will not let him rest. At length, without the knowledge of his parents, he sets off for Delphi, to obtain satisfaction from Apollo; but the god, instead of answering his question, announces

to him as his destiny, that *he shall wed his own mother, beget a race
hideous to mankind, and be the slayer of his own father.* Cf. 788 sqq.,
994 sqq. Having received this oracle, he resolves, hard as it may be to
him, never again to see his parents (999), but to turn his back forever
upon his Corinthian home, in order to escape from the doom predicted
by Apollo; for that he is truly the son of the affectionate fosterers of his
infancy, he thinks he can no longer doubt. Alone he wanders,
unknowing whither, through Phocis. At this same time (114 sqq.) it
chanced that Laïus was on his way from Thebes to Apollo's oracle at
Delphi, we know not upon what errand. At the point where the high-
roads from Delphi and from Daulia (733 sq.) meet in a narrow pass, the
wanderer is met by an old man riding in a chariot, the driver at the time
leading the horses. Both with violence attempt to force him out of the
way. Being enraged, he deals the driver a blow, and then essays to
pursue his way quietly. The old man, however, watches his
opportunity, and at the moment when Oedipus is in the act of passing
the chariot, with his double goad deals him a blow right on the middle
of his head. Upon this Oedipus instantly strikes him a fatal blow with
his walking-staff; he falls backward from the chariot and dies. In the
heat of his rage, Oedipus slays the other attendants also. So at least he
believes: but one of them escapes, and to save himself from the
reproach of a cowardly flight, on his arrival in Thebes relates that a
band of robbers had fallen upon the party, 122 sq. This falsehood was
indispensable for the poet, in order that Oedipus might not be allowed
to come too soon upon the right track; so likewise was the
representation that only one escaped, whose account of the matter could
not be contradicted by other witnesses.

Proceeding on his way, Oedipus arrives in the neighborhood of
Thebes a short time after the escaped attendant has brought the
intelligence of the violent death of Laïus. Here, at that precise time, the
Sphinx had her lair, a monster who, seizing on all that passed that way,
propounded her enigma, and if they could not solve it, hurled them
headlong from the rock, thereby decimating the city. Her enigma is
couched by an unknown poet in the following verses:—

> Ἔστι δίπουν ἐπὶ γῆς καὶ τετράπον, οὗ μία φωνή,
> καὶ τρίπον· ἀλλάσσει δὲ φυὴν μόνον ὅσσ' ἐπὶ γαῖαν
> ἑρπετὰ κινεῖται ἀνά τ' αἰθέρα καὶ κατὰ πόντον.
> ἀλλ' ὁπόταν πλείστοισιν ἐρειδόμενον ποσὶ βαίῃ,
> ἔνθα τάχος γυίοισιν ἀφαυρότατον πέλει αὑτοῦ,

Oedipus also passes by the mountain of the Sphinx, a stranger, and
not as yet apprised by the Thebans concerning her proceedings; yet he
intrepidly tries his fortune, and solves the Enigma of Man, whereupon

the monster throws herself from the rock. This λύσις also has been put in verse:—

Κλῦθι καὶ οὐκ ἐθέλουσα, κακόπτερε Μοῦσα θανόντων,
φωνῆς ἡμετέρης σὸν τέλος ἀμπλακίης ·
ἄνθρωπον κατέλεξας, ὃς ἡνίκα γαῖαν ἐφέρπει,
πρῶτον ἔφυ τετράπους νήπιος ἐκ λαγόνων.
γηραλέος δὲ πέλων τρίτατον πόδα βάκτρον ἐρείδει,
αὐχένα φορτίζων, γήραϊ καμπτόμενος.

He is recognized as the savior of the state, and receives, together with the throne left vacant by the death of Laïus, the widow of the king as his wife, and now as king in Thebes passes many years in undisturbed prosperity. Jocasta bears him four children; the city honors him as the greatest and best of men, who, not without the special favor of the gods, overcame the Sphinx, 33 sqq. But suddenly, after long years (561), the happiness which the gods awarded him is disturbed by a blight upon the fruits of the earth, and a pestilence on man and beast,—the punishment sent by Apollo because of the neglected expiation of the old murder. In his vigilant care for the city, Oedipus has sent the man who stands next to himself and to the throne, his wife's brother Creon, with whom he has ever lived in undisturbed friendship (590 sqq.), to Delphi, for the purpose of invoking, in this trying emergency likewise, the aid of the Pythian god. At this point begins the action of the tragedy.

Prologos, 1-150. The distress having risen to the highest point, the whole population, not as yet acquainted with the measures taken by the king, has formed suppliant processions to the sanctuaries of the gods. Those who are the most in need of help, gray-headed old priests, young children, and chosen youths, repair to the palace of their sovereign on the Cadmeia. Oedipus, as a father, comes forth among his children, to inform himself of the purpose of this assembly, and to express his readiness to aid them to the utmost of his power. The priest of Zeus, whose age and dignity call him to be spokesman, depicts the general distress as the cause of their thus betaking themselves to him, the approved deliverer, who owes it to himself to be still the savior of the state. Deeply moved, Oedipus replies to this confiding and honorable address, that without waiting for any exhortation from others, he has of his own accord taken thought for all that can be done for the deliverance of his people from a calamity which indeed presses upon him above all others. Creon has been sent to Delphi, and whatever the god may order for the deliverance of the city, that will he do willingly.

To the joy of all, Creon appears. At the express wish of Oedipus, he announces, in the presence of the whole assembly, that Apollo peremptorily demands from the citizens that *the slayer of Laïus, who is*

living in the land, be either banished or put to death, seeing this
polluted person has brought upon Thebes the present calamity.
Hereupon, while the points of moment for the connection of the fable
are brought out by a series of questions and answers, Oedipus learns
that Laïus upon a time having left Thebes upon a θεωρία,—with what
object, and to what oracle, is purposely not specified,—never returned;
it was only known that he had been slain by a band of robbers. That no
search was made at the time for the doer of this deed was caused by the
Sphinx, who obliged them to confine their thoughts to their own
immediate concerns. Oedipus, all unsuspecting, is prompt with his
resolve to lose not a moment in executing the divine injunction. Needs
must he himself apprehend that so daring a murderer, who, he fancies,
must have been set on by political opponents in Thebes, may lay hands
on him likewise! He then bids the assembled suppliants withdraw, and
appoints one of his attendants to summon the principal citizens of
Thebes, as he will leave nothing unattempted that may lead to the
desired end.

Oedipus and Creon go within the palace. Creon advises him to
send a messenger for Tiresias, which he does, and after a time,
impatient at his not arriving, he despatches a second. The citizens,
whom the king has summoned, appear before the palace. As the age,
sex, and position of the choreutae are for the most part chosen to match
the protagonists, so here the χώρας ἄνακτες form the Chorus, as in the
Oed. Col. old men, in the Electra maidens, in the Ajax comrades in
war, in the Philoctetes mariners. The deficiency in mental acumen and
insight into the bearings of the events which appears in our choreutae
was necessary for the poet in the management of the action; they must
needs be men of limited minds and slow perception, that they may not,
any more than their king, be able to see through the true connection and
dependence of the incidents, and may still enter into and echo their
master's tone of feeling. At the same time, their quietude makes them
well adapted for thoughtful appreciation of the stormy passions which
rave before them. As they take their place in the orchestra around the
thymele, they strike up the Parodos, 151-215. Aware of Creon's return,
but as yet unacquainted with the purport of the oracle brought by him,
with their expectation wrought up to the highest pitch, they invoke, in
solemn rhythm, the chiefest of Thebes' tutelary deities, and depict in
vivid colors the tribulations of their city; and then once more supplicate
the succor of the gods, severally invoking them in long detail. By thus
separating the Chorus from the ἱκέται, Sophocles gets a natural
occasion for letting Oedipus, by his announcement of the oracle, and of
the measures which he has taken accordingly, exhibit himself in all his
security and consciousness of innocence; while, at the same time, his
address shows how heinous he considers the crime to be, and how
earnestly he takes the injunction of the god.

First Epeisodion, 216-462. Oedipus, who, shortly before the close of the choral song, again appears, takes up the concluding thought, and bids the Chorus depend upon his active zeal, to which the command of the god has appointed its course of proceeding. But in his haste to obey the god, he neglects to acquaint the Chorus, in the first place, with that which they so ardently desired to know,—the purport of the oracle. This they learn only by way of corollary, 242, in quite general terms. For Oedipus, hurried on unawares by a supernatural excitement, begins with emphatically protesting his own utter ignorance, until now, of that which he is about to communicate, thereby explaining how it comes that he, hitherto the wise counsellor in time of need, is obliged, for this time, to have recourse to the help of the citizens. Upon these he solemnly enjoins it as a duty in every way to aid in the discovery of the slayer of Laïus, upon whom he imprecates the heaviest curse, should he remain secret, while he commends the innocent population to the abiding protection of the gods. Upon the spectator, apprised from the outset of the real bearings of the events, the impassioned address of Oedipus must have had a thrilling effect. His speech, now quiet and gentle, now vehement and impetuous, becomes most impassioned at the very point where he imprecates upon the perpetrator and the abettor the evil that falls back upon himself.

The Chorus protests its innocence and ignorance, but counsels to send for Tiresias. For this Oedipus has already taken care. In his disquietude, he marvels that the seer, though two messengers have been sent, has not yet made his appearance. The choragus then meditatively remarks that the story once current in the mouths of the people leads to nothing. Oedipus, not despising any, even the slightest trace, bids him tell what this was; but he learns nothing more than what Creon had already communicated as the report of the escaped attendant, that Laïus was slain by robbers, or, as it is here said with a nearer approximation to the truth, by travellers.

Then comes the blind seer Tiresias, whose mental eye has long clearly seen through all, and from whom the Chorus, with confidence, hopes that he will bring the doer of the deed to light; as in fact does come to pass, though in a manner wholly unexpected. Oedipus also expects speedy deliverance through Tiresias; and so it comes about that the very man on whom the entire population had built all its hope looks for help to the blind seer, who yet in the times of the Sphinx had held his peace!

The king welcomes the prophet with most honorable expressions of entire confidence, lays before him the purport of the oracle, and calls upon him to put forth all the resources of his art for the deliverance of the city. Tiresias, embarrassed, and repenting of his coming, adjures him to desist: his knowledge profits him not! It has been out of forbearance to the well-deserving ruler that he has so long shut up the secret in his own breast, and even now only upon provocation does he make the disclosures which follow. The king importunes, the seer persists in his refusal: let him be wroth if he will,—it will all come to light without a word from him! By degrees the already excited king is wrought up into a towering passion. Conscious that he himself is doing everything to carry out the injunction of the god, it exasperates him that Tiresias, having the power to help, refuses his aid. In bitter altercation he gives vent to the accusation that Tiresias himself was the instigator of the murder. Upon this, the seer, himself by this time angered, declares that Oedipus is the murderer. But the king, his suspicions once having been roused, listens no longer to the child of night. Tiresias adds yet further—and in this Oedipus, in a calmer state of mind, could not have failed to perceive an echo of his own old oracle—that he is cohabiting with his nearest kindred in horrible intimacy. But no sooner has the seer appealed to Apollo, who will presently bring the matter to an issue, than a new suspicion adds to the infatuation which already possesses the blinded king. At the very hearing of Apollo, it flashes upon him that Creon—the bearer of the oracle from Delphi—is at the bottom of the matter, and that the seer, for love of base gain, has been acting upon his suggestions. This thought, rendered in some measure plausible by the fact that it was Creon who had advised the sending for the seer, in the impetuous Oedipus becomes at once a certainty; and the rather as, on the very first hearing of the matter, it had occurred to him that the murderer must have been set on by political motives. Following it up, he indignantly accuses Creon (who in company with Oedipus had left the stage at 146, and is not now present) as a conspirator with whom Tiresias is leagued to compass his overthrow. Now he scoffs at that which he has just before so highly extolled,—the prophetic skill of Tiresias,—a man who, for all his pretensions, had no power to help in the time of the Sphinx! His confidence shaken in all whom he had revered and loved, Oedipus, once so discreet, now sets up his γνώμη against the τέχνη of the professed seer, with all its infallibility, and menaces both the conspirators with the punishment they deserve.

Tiresias now, for the second time, reveals in connected detail (412-428) the calamities which await Oedipus, living, as he does, in most disastrous unconsciousness of the horrors by which he is surrounded. In a burst of wrath, he bids the seer be gone. The latter, in replying to the taunt of his having uttered nothing but follies, with the answer, "Thy parents thought me wise," has launched at the king a new shaft, so that from this time the painful recollection of the old unexplained mystery of his extraction mixes itself up with his present solicitude. With his demand for enlightenment Tiresias declines to comply, but darkly hints that this day, ere it close, will explain all. Then, before he withdraws, he for the third time expresses himself concerning the murderer in terms awfully enigmatical, but still clearly calculated to remind

Oedipus of the old oracle; not now, however, as before, addressing the king himself, and expressly mentioning him by name, but speaking as if concerning a third person. He concludes with the words, "If these sayings be not made good, then Oedipus shall say that Tiresias knows nothing of the art which he professes." The king, also, for whom each fancied access of insight but deepens his blindness, retires into the palace. The spectator has now before him, in all its completeness, the prodigious contrast between the outward semblance and the reality. The truth which Oedipus desires to have he thrusts from him, and falls at variance, moreover, with the seer, until now his well-wisher, and with his most faithful friend. It sets this contrast in a sharper light that the Chorus is involved in the same delusions with its lord. This short-sightedness of the Chorus appears immediately in bold relief in the First Stasimon, 463-512.

Second Epeisodion, 513-862, with a Kommos, 649-697, with interposed trimeters. With great art the following scene is brought on by the dialogue with Tiresias. Creon, informed of the accusation raised against him by Oedipus, indignantly appears and endeavors to learn from the Chorus whether that harsh charge had indeed been made by a sane mind. But while the Chorus, in its loyal attachment to its lord, considerately shrinks from satisfying the inquiry, the king himself appears, and so the full explanation is reserved for the dialogue between the parties concerned. He gives his wife's brother a rough reception. To have the audacity to come into his presence,—him, his detected murderer and the robber of his throne! Creon must needs regard him a coward or fool, if he thinks to delude him, or supposes that his plottings will not be promptly met! Creon, on the other hand, advises Oedipus first to look calmly into the facts of the case. And now the king, to make his grounds sure, commences an examination, point by point. He asks whether it was not Creon's suggestion that he should send for the seer. This being answered in the affirmative, he asks whether Tiresias had ever, in former times, pointed at him as the guilty person. If he, who now all on the sudden thinks fit to mark him as the murderer, has before this held his peace, it is to him a demonstrated fact that he was prompted by Creon, who coveted the throne. The more conclusive Oedipus deems this inference, the more firmly does he here once more fix himself in his error.

Hereupon Creon, having first shown how near he stands to Oedipus and his queen, goes into a long train of argument, wishing to demonstrate, by a rational discussion of all the circumstances, how utterly absurd it would be in him to entertain the ambitious design upon the throne of which he is accused. If Oedipus can convict him of having a crafty understanding with Tiresias, he protests himself ready to die a shameful death. Without listening to this oath, or taking heed to the pacific admonitions of the Chorus, the king insists that Creon must die as a traitor.

At this point the choragus, 631 sqq., announces the approach of Jocasta, whom the altercation has called from the palace. She bids them for shame desist, in the midst of the general distress, from stirring up private quarrels. Upon this, Oedipus lays before her his impeachment of Creon, and the latter by the most solemn oath again asseverates his innocence. It is only upon the most urgent entreaties of his wife and of the choreutse, that the king lets Creon go,—not in the least convinced that he has wronged his wife's brother,—but with the express declaration that he will never cease to hate him. Creon withdraws, protesting that his sovereign has misjudged him, whereas the whole city knows that he is still what he always was; and he ominously predicts that Oedipus will be pained by the thought of his injustice, when once his passion is allayed.

Upon Creon's departure, at Jocasta's desire, her husband relates the occasion of the quarrel, the Chorus having vainly besought him to let the matter rest. Creon, he says, would fain make him out to be the murderer; so little is he able to free himself from his preconceived opinion that Tiresias was suborned by him to accuse him of the deed! With shrewd womanly art, Jocasta now sets herself to convince her husband, already more than enough entangled in a web of self-deception, that the vaunted science of the seers is not worth heeding. There was an old oracle given to Laïus which was so far from receiving its fulfilment, that foreign robbers, as the story goes,—this then she trusts implicitly, without much questioning its grounds or want of grounds,—slew him on the common high-way: as for her child, it was exposed immediately after its birth. Thus was the response of the ministers of the Delphian temple put to shame!

But here the punishment follows close on the heels of the blasphemy. This very story, which was meant to set her husband's mind quite at rest as regarded one oracle, by the instance of another oracle which was falsified by the event, produces just the opposite result. The words of the seer, so plain and pointed, remained an enigma for Oedipus: now one casual harmless word arrests his attention and staggers him in the confidence he has thus far felt. Now begins the wonderfully contrived περιπέτεια; a faint presentiment of the truth arises in the hero's mind, but the poet has the skill yet for a long time to retard the full discovery. Not only now but again and again hereafter this same tragical effect attends the process of the discovery, that the gradual uplifting of the veil is effected by the very persons who are endeavoring to relieve the hero's mind of its growing anxieties.

When, namely, Jocasta mentions that Laïus was slain πρὸς τριπλαῖς ἁμαξιτοῖς,—a spot where there would naturally be frequent encounters of people coming from different directions,—Oedipus eagerly catches at this description of the locality, and inquires whither the pass led, how long ago this occurrence befell, how old Laïus was, and of what appearance. When all tallies with his own old adventure, an indescribable anxiety takes possession of his mind, lest after all Tiresias be found to see but too truly. For even the number of the attendants accords; and now he desires Jocasta to send with all speed for the slave who had then returned, that he may gain the satisfaction he needs from him. The slave had recognized in the highly praised deliverer of the city, and husband of the queen, the slayer of his lord. As the sight of him must ever remind him of his falsehood about the band of robbers, he had withdrawn from Thebes. Of the fact that the new king was the son of Laïus, he had no knowledge. It was a necessary contrivance of the poet's that the slave, whom Oedipus had omitted to summon in the first instance (118), should not be present, yet not too remote; and the mention by Jocasta, just at this point, where the elucidation of the mystery lies so close at hand, of the reason why he wished to be dismissed into the country, is ominously significant.

Jocasta, having as yet no foreboding of the ground of her husband's anxiety, wishes to learn what it is; whereupon Oedipus, who in Thebes was universally held to be the son of Polybus, frankly relates his juvenile history, and the adventure in the σχιστὴ ὁδός. If the old man whom he slew was Laïus, he must bewail himself as of all mortal men the most hated of the gods, since upon him must then light all the heavy curses which he has openly denounced upon the murderer. In his contemplation of this contingency, he is still so blind that he bewails the hard fate which makes it impossible for him, if the case be so, ever to return to his old home and his beloved parents at Corinth, if he would not incur the yet worse misery of fulfilling the old oracle by slaying Polybus and wedding Merope. At every step which the hero takes toward the truth, the poet has the art to excite afresh, and with more intensity, the ἔλεος and φόβος of the spectator. The way in which, step by step, the truth comes out, is managed with inimitable art. As yet the hero's misgiving is limited to the milder half of his disastrous condition, the apprehension that he may have been the slayer of the royal husband of his wife; his parents he innocently assumes to be living in Corinth, and dreads the possible fulfilment of that which lies long years behind him in the past! Even for that milder object of his apprehension, dreadful as the contemplation of it is to the high-souled king, he has still a ray of hope.

If, namely, the herdsman shall persist in his story that *robbers* were the slayers of the old king, he, a solitary individual, cannot be the culprit. Jocasta goes yet further; even if the herdsman should vary in his tale, this need not trouble him. Loxias plainly declared that her husband should fall by the hand of his own son; but this son perished long before his father. Consequently she will never believe in prophecy and divination. Meanwhile she will send forthwith for the herdsman; until then let Oedipus with her enter their palace.

Second Stasimon, 863-910. The pious old men, deeply offended by the daring levity shown by Jocasta in her avowed disregard of the utterances of the gods, and by the godless way in which she has spoken of her past life, especially the icy coldness of heart which she betrayed in her account of the exposure of her infant, pray to Zeus that he will confirm the truth of the oracle given to Laïus. Armed with the holy primeval laws of religion and morality, they contend for their inviolable sanctity, unchecked by any misgiving that the object they would obtain by their prayer is indeed none other than the speedy overthrow of the king to whom they still adhere with the same devoted loyalty as ever.

Third Epeisodion, 911-1085. Suddenly Jocasta comes forth, and explains that a fancy has taken her to offer to the gods. Need teaches prayer. Within doors she cannot breathe freely; while Oedipus, a prey to boundless dejection, persists in rejecting all that she can suggest for the quieting of his disturbed mind, and lends an ear only to the most alarming representations. Jocasta draws near to the altar of the very god whose utterances she has but now again treated with contempt, and whose wisdom she will presently, on the first seeming lull of the storm, once more, with her usual levity, turn into derision. The impression made by the language of the profane queen—irreligious even in her devotions—tells with the greater effect by contrast with the loftiness and purity of the sentiments to which the magnificent ode, whose last accents have but just died away, has attuned the minds of the spectators.

Apparently, the god instantly grants the prayer, that the reality, when it comes, may be all the more crushing. A messenger appears from Corinth, who, in the belief that he is the bringer of joyful tidings, shows a cheerful bearing. Polybus is dead; and he, in hope of rich reward, has immediately set off on his journey hither to be the first bearer of the tidings to Oedipus, whom, as he says he has heard, the Corinthians intend to make their king. On hearing this, Jocasta triumphantly calls out her husband. There now are the oracles again falsified! And now even the pious king, with this new fact before him, cannot forbear to chime in with her exultation, and emboldens himself to speak disparagingly of oracle and flight of birds. True, upon recollecting the studied ambiguity and equivocal character of the language of oracles, it occurs to him—always ready-minded, and always at fault in the direction of his reflections—that Polybus' death may have been caused by grief for the loss of him, in which case the god will yet be true, and he, in a sense, the slayer of his father. So difficult does he find it to accord with Jocasta's tone of feeling, and so much does his pious mind revolt from her profane levity, that rather than doubt the truth of the divine words, he chooses to take refuge in casuistical refinements. And then forthwith the other part of the old oracle falls heavily on his soul,—that he should become the husband of his mother. Jocasta, indeed, is prompt with her woman's counsel; one must drive such crotchets out of one's head; that is the only way to live comfortably, 977 sqq. But the messenger from Corinth, to whom Oedipus makes known the cause of his fear, hastes, with the best intentions, to relieve him of his distress. Polybus was of no kin to Oedipus; from his own hands the pair received the boy. Laïus' herdsman, who handed the child over to him upon a time when they were together in Cithaeron, would be able to throw further light upon the subject. The Chorus recognizes in this herdsman the very man who has been summoned to explain the circumstances of the old king's death. For he it was that had accompanied Laïus and escaped with the tidings of his death to Thebes. Jocasta, the scales now at once falling from her eyes, adjures Oedipus to desist from further investigation; but this he peremptorily declines. Upon this Jocasta hurries off from the scene, with words which portend some frightful resolve on her part. Oedipus, again misapprehending the true bearings of the case, imagines that Jocasta's vanity is wounded; that she fears he may be found to be of ignoble extraction. For his part, he will not rest until he gets at the whole truth of his parentage; come what will, he regards himself as a son of Tyche, who has made him small and great. Nothing daunts the strong hero; before all things he will learn the full truth.

A Hyporchema, 1086-1109, of cheerful character serves, just before the catastrophe, to shed a last gleam of light upon the gathering gloom, while the Chorus, wholly entering into the tone of the protagonist, pictures to itself that Oedipus may perchance be the child of a god by some mountain-nymph of Cithaeron.

Fourth Epeisodion, 1110-1185. The herdsman for whose coming Oedipus has longed appears, and is recognized by the Corinthian as the person from whose hands he received the child. Of the attack made upon Laïus by a number of robbers, which was the point on which the king desired satisfaction when he was urgent to have this man summoned, we hear no more, now that matters have taken a new turn, in consequence of which all is cleared up at once so soon as the hero's origin is brought to light. The other recalls to the recollection of the Theban herdsman the days they spent together on the mountains, and thinks to give him a joyful surprise with the discovery that the boy whom the other handed over to him is none other than the king before whom they stand. The horrified Theban is forced by violent menaces to confess that Jocasta herself consigned the child to his hands for destruction, moved to this by fear of an oracle which foretold that the child would one day slay his father. That he would also wed his mother was no part of the oracle given to Laïus; this was only prophesied to Oedipus. Now first the whole hideous reality, in all its parts, is laid bare before the eyes of the king. Having, with a bitter cry, bid farewell to the light of day, and summed up with pregnant brevity the chain of horrors through which Tiresias so well saw, he rushes into the house.

Third Stasimon, 1186-1222. The Chorus having contemplated *the sudden vicissitudes of all earthly things*, then follows,

The Exodos, 1223 to the end. Inserted in this is a second Kommos, 1313-1368, intermixed with trimeters by the Chorus.

An exangelus gives a relation of the portentous horrors which have befallen in the palace. Jocasta has strangled herself in the thalamus; Oedipus, like a maniac, with loud yell, has burst in, and with Jocasta's golden clasps bored out both his eyes, to escape the sight of his misery and misdeeds. So, says the messenger, has measureless wretchedness entered in, where once dwelt high prosperity.

Then, to show to the Thebans in his horribly mutilated condition— for which the description given by the messenger has prepared them— the unhappy sufferer, whose noble spirit, as it never knew concealment, so now will have no disguises, the palace-doors fly open, and Oedipus totters forth. He now bewails alternately with the Chorus, without reproaching any other than himself, his self-inflicted blindness, and his disastrous destiny. Anon, collecting himself, he speaks (from 1369) of the fearful punishment he has inflicted upon himself; he weighs the circumstances which made it impossible for him any longer to behold the light. He concludes with the prayer that the Chorus will thrust him out of the land, or make away with him. So little is he content with the punishment which, in his frenzy, he has inflicted upon himself, until the oracle of the Pythian god concerning the slayer of Laïus be also satisfied to the uttermost.

The Chorus refers him to Creon, whom it sees approaching. During the minority of the sons, Creon is the natural successor to the throne, as Sophocles makes the hero forthwith abdicate the sovereignty. So, after the lapse of a few hours, Creon, without doing anything toward it himself, has through Oedipus' own proceedings attained to the very dignity which he was previously accused of unrighteously affecting! The unhappy king, who has now seen how greatly he was deceived in the suspicion he was led to entertain of his old friend, is alarmed at the announcement of Creon's approach. But, as in the Ajax, Ulysses, after the death of his enemy, comes forward as the noble vindicator of his merits, and in the Philoctetes the position of Neoptolemus relative to Philoctetes in the course of the action undergoes a complete revolution, so the relation of Creon to Oedipus takes an unexpected turn; for Creon, entirely vindicated by the events, comes forward as a sympathizing friend and helper in time of need, and makes it plain that he has retained no recollection of the offence. In the first place he desires them immediately to withdraw from the light of day the shocking spectacle of the unhappy sufferer; but when Oedipus addresses to him also the request that, agreeably with the dictate of Apollo, he may be banished, he bids him wait patiently for the decision of the god, which he holds himself bound to seek once more before taking any further measures. Submitting to this arrangement, and having commended to Creon's pious care the obsequies of his wretched sister, on his own behalf he has nothing more to ask but that he may be thrust out to Cithaeron, the place once appointed by his parents for his grave; only the thought of his two poor daughters weighs heavily upon his fatherly heart; as for the sons, they are already able to help themselves. The latter he does not ask to see,—their character as godless men is fixed in the myth,—but the maidens, whom he dearly loves, he would fain embrace once more. Even for this, Creon, who knows the heartfelt love which their unhappy father has ever borne them, has taken thought. Cordially thanking him for this kindness, Oedipus pathetically surveys all the painful circumstances which may await the orphaned maidens, who, in the innocence of their hearts, incapable of comprehending the horrors of the situation, stand mutely by. With warm affection he commends them to the faithful guardianship of Creon, who must supply to them the place of a father. So the poet manages to give to the horrors of the drama a milder close, and to afford the spectator a consolatory glance into the future.

Upon this Creon bids him go in: if such be the will of the god, he will surely obtain his desire of quitting the land.

In the concluding trochees, the Chorus points out how in the man who but now was extolled as wisest and greatest of men, the maxim of Solon is verified, that *no mortal must be accounted happy until one has learned by experience whether his good fortune will be faithful to him unto the end of his days.* Undoubtedly this is the most evident idea that suggests itself to us in our contemplation of the Drama of the Fall of Oedipus: as accordingly it is carried out at greater length in the last stasimon, and is also brought forward by the exangelus, 1282 sqq. Here also that reflection of Ulysses in the Ajax is in place, ὁρῶ γὰρ ἡμᾶς οὐδὲν ὄντας ἄλλο πλὴν εἴδωλ᾿, ὅσοιπερ ζῶμεν, ἢ κούφη σκιά. But it would be a great mistake to imagine that Sophocles intended in this gnome to put at once into our hands the idea which his drama was meant to enforce, and in which all should find its central unity. The world unfolded in this drama exhibits a portraiture much too individually marked for any such conception; its relations, bearings, characters, are far too special to admit of our spanning with this formula the poetical conception of the drama considered in its essence. The vicissitude exhibited is but the external consequence of inward contradictions; it lights upon Oedipus, who seems to have been singled out by fate as the ball of its caprice. His entire life is one continued oscillation between unmitigated opposites; his endeavor and will stand to the actual result in the most crying contradiction; where he strives after the best, he works misery; where he thinks to go right cleverly to work, his sagacity is ever at fault, while, if he does hit the truth, it is but by accident, unconsciously and unavailingly. The language of the oracles he misinterprets throughout: the Sphinx's riddle he solves while yet his own being is, and continues to be, to him an enigma. Personally conscious of no guilt, he becomes entangled in the most disastrous destinies: circumstances, seemingly the most unfavorable, lend him a hand to unlooked-for success. As these contrasts are seen in that part of his life which is external to the action of our drama, so in the drama itself they lie before us in all their asperity. The deep tragedy of the play lies in the very circumstance that a terrible utterance of the god receives its fulfilment at the very point where Oedipus has not had a remote conception of it; that where he most zealously and with keen eye explores the traces of another's guilt, he accelerates the downfall of his own prosperity, and puts a sharper edge to his unhappy destiny by blind precipitancy in consequence of his seeming wisdom; that he attains the object to which he has bent his mind day and night, the salvation of the state, but that the new deliverance of the city he has once happily delivered is his own destruction. The pestilence which gave occasion to the discovery of the truth ceases; the sorely visited and yet innocent city breathes freely again, and the perdition falls upon the very man who at the opening of the play, alone together with those belonging to him, seemed exempt from the general destruction, of which, nevertheless, he was the cause.

The higher Oedipus seems to stand in outward felicity, in endowments of understanding and heart, the vaster the separation, as the drama develops it, between truth and semblance. He was worthy of a better fate: but even before he was begotten he was chosen to be the unnatural instrument of the divine vengeance upon his father and his mother: their transgression should thereby undergo the severest retribution. He takes the life of him who gave him life; she, the mother who would put her child out of the way, conceives children by this her child. It is she who undergoes the most hideous fate, because it was she who seduced Laïus to slight the prohibition of Apollo, and because she thereafter stifled the natural voice of a mother's love.

If now we trace more closely the contrasts in the hero's life and destinies, as Sophocles has carried them out in minutest detail, we are met by the wide chasm between the outward welfare of the son of Tyche (1080 sqq.) and the misery once for all doomed to him by the gods from his very birth. Scarce three days old is he, when by the hands of the parents—who nevertheless longed for heirs—he is ruthlessly maimed, and consigned to destruction. Given over to a foreign shepherd to be brought up as his child, he is presented as a gift to a childless pair in ἀφνειὸς Κόρινθος, and by their consentient love is reared—he, the foreign-born, the maimed foundling, the child of unknown parents—as own offspring of royal parents, as heir of an illustrious throne. A mere chance, in a party met for pleasure, shatters the juvenile happiness of the youth who in the eyes of every man ranked as first of the Corinthian citizens. Thirsting for the clearing up of his doubts, he thinks to betake him to the surest source; but concerning the past, which he wishes to know, Apollo is silent, and intimates all that is most horrible concerning the future, for which he was not questioned. He would fain secure himself against the fulfilment of the oracle. What it is in the power of man to do, he does. But while the homeless pilgrim wanders lonely and without an aim into the country where he may be farthest removed from his Corinthian parents, he slays his true father in an encounter wherein he was justified in using violence in self-defence. For that father purposes at the cross-roads also to slay him, unknown, whom as a child he had wittingly sought to put out of the way; but this time also his attempt miscarries, that the will of the gods may be done. Chance leads the young man to Thebes: he solves the enigma at which all before him had labored in vain; and this very fortune hurls him into the deepest abyss of ruin. The community of his native city rewards him with the vacant throne and the hand of his mother. Then, long undisturbed domestic and public felicity. But the gods leave no sin unpunished, be it early or late; and blood once shed, above all the blood of a father shed by the hand of a child, may not remain unavenged, be the culprit accountable or not. Apollo sends blight and pestilence upon the city which harbors the blood-guilty one. Again Oedipus betakes him to the same god who has once prophesied to him, and whom he must needs regard as the author of his prosperity, seeing that his oracle, by warning him against returning to Corinth, has been the means of his present exaltation. At last, when he has wandered through many a maze of error, his eyes— and this is the matter of our play—are opened. Ere this, he who solved the Enigma of Humanity is left, concerning his own human relations, to grope his way, even to the hideous catastrophe, in utter darkness. It is a point of deep significance—and this formed from the first a marked trait of the popular fiction—that he takes revenge upon the bodily eye for the blindness of his mind; that the darkened mind in the midst of light may have its counterpart in the seeing mind and darkened body.

The character of the Sophoclean Oedipus is spotless, as in fact he stands there in the popular fiction,—the innocent victim of ruthless destiny. From his youth up he has confidingly surrendered himself to the guidance of the bright god of Delphi, and with him will he stand or fall (145). Passionate he is, no doubt, else were he no subject for tragedy. But the poet is ever anxious to let it be seen that even his excesses spring from noble impulses. To him, as the prologue and many other passages of the play declare, the public weal is supreme above all other considerations. Conscious of the purest aims, and convinced that he is serving the god, he becomes harsh and suspicious toward those whose proceedings seem not to be directed to the same end: he loses his steadfastness of self-command and self-consistency, thereby aggravating the miserable lot, which cannot be, nor is meant to be, referred to this as its cause. Without these darker shades in the portraiture of the hero, otherwise sagacious in insight and mild in disposition, yet ever putting himself palpably in the wrong, the dramatic action would lose in inner truthfulness and consistency. As it is, the sentiment in the Antigone, 622-624, becomes applicable to him, τὸ κακὸν δοκεῖν ποτ' ἐσθλὸν τῷδ' ἔμμεν ὅτῳ φρένας θεὸς ἄγει πρὸς ἄταν. So, likewise, and only so, the way in which the poet has contrived, with wonderful skill, to retard the catastrophe acquires its ground of psychological truth. The passion, too, is quite natural; it is, as Oedipus says (334), enough to provoke a stone to see Tiresias so reluctant to serve his god. And, as if it were not enough that he has in this way thrown the king off his self-possession, the seer must needs also awaken the old uncomfortable feelings about his parentage, and moreover gives him occasion to impute a criminal design to Creon, though Creon has not the slightest notion of the true state of the case. And then, when all at once the seer turns round and impeaches him as the murderer, is it not enough to set him ablaze with indignation? For he could not possibly see that Tiresias had all these years kept silence only out of respect for his noble qualities as a man, and for the wisdom with which as king he was guiding the state. And Tiresias, likewise, himself loses his temper, and is forced out of the dignified repose of his sacred character. In all else Oedipus is throughout a grand, heroic figure; not, indeed, to be scanned by the rule of later times, but one of the forms of the gigantesque olden time, and of that hard, granite-like generation with which old Nestor conversed in his younger days. In particular, the princely stock of the Cadmeiones is characterized by a lofty sternness and stubbornness which in fact makes the traditions of that race stand in such marked contrast to those of the Achaian houses. If to others Oedipus is harsh, his greatest harshness is to himself; the utmost severity of punishment that could of right be visited upon him, he outdoes by the measureless vengeance he takes upon his innocent eyes. For such is the length to which the tragic illusion is carried, that in the state into which his feelings are wrought up, he does not pause to examine the facts of his case in their proper characters, but holds himself alone responsible for all that through him has come to pass.

Oedipus, then, the hated of the gods, is a standing example of that article of the popular creed according to which a man, in spite of the purest intentions, may fail utterly, only because he is an object of aversion to the gods; a faith which took its rise from observation of the enormous disparity which is so often seen between men's merits and their fate. Let it not be thought that this conception of the Oedipus is not that which in a moral point of view would commend itself to the religious mind of a Sophocles. It should be remembered that for the basis of this surpassingly wonderful creation of his genius, he found the story ready-made to his hand. To settle the odds of guilt and punishment could never be the task he set himself, unless he would mar the whole sense of the fable. Further, it should be considered that Oedipus, however pure in his own person, bore with him an inherited sin; for as, in the faith of the ancients, the misdeeds of the parents were often left unpunished in them, to be visited on children and children's children, so likewise the parents' sin imparts itself to the children, and weighs upon them; nay, even in the common intercourse of life, the sin of the impure passes by contagion to the pure, and draws them together into the same destruction.

All things considered, the fundamental idea of the drama can be no other than this: *For mortal man, be he ever so good, not all the watchfulness he can use in pondering his steps will suffice to guard him against misgoings; not all the penetration he can exercise in the discovery of the right will avail for his good, if once the love of the gods be withheld. Be the outward semblance ever so dazzling, the longer the respite the deeper the perdition into which the gods, by inexorable necessity, will at last hurl the ἐχθρδαίμων.* In Oedipus we have the impersonation of the utter impotence of man when put upon his own resources. What has it availed him that the gods, by fore-announcement of his destiny, have given him a look into the future which lies before him? Destiny has spread her toils for him, and he falls into them at the very point where he thinks right cleverly to evade them, and to secure his safety. That it is the duty of man humbly to submit himself to a higher guidance, was the general popular faith; this lowly resignation expresses itself in the fact of their praying to the gods that they would grant the power to do that which was right. Of the too harsh destiny which lights upon Oedipus, a righteous compensation is afforded in his end: this is the idea presented in the counterpart of our play, the Oedipus at Colonus, which at the same time affords the fullest proof that the conception of the Oedipus as here stated was, and must have been, that which Sophocles from the first intended.

The parts assigned to all the other persons of the drama seem intended, from first to last, to furnish motives to the procedure of the protagonist, and to draw out his character in a stronger light. In particular, Jocasta stands there beside her noble husband, with a mind how differently constituted! It is her maxim to live for the day. Should anything occur to disturb the god-forgetting tenor of her course, she seeks only to thrust it aside as soon as possible. The earnestness of Oedipus in learning the truth, regardless of what may follow, is to her alien. For truth and right she cares less than for present comfort. To her first husband, reckless of the divine warning he has received, she, having by her arts infatuated him, bears a child, and then, fearing the consequences, without more ado, puts it out of her sight: whether it was really destroyed, of this she had no certainty. Set at rest for the moment, she asks no further questions: gods and oracles give her no concern, save at the actual pinch of need; at other times, her daring levity carries her even to the length of reckless blasphemy. Her marriage with the young Corinthian prince makes her oblivious of the sacred duty of bringing to light her husband's murderers. The old slave she willingly dismisses, because his presence must continually remind her of her child, and of her former husband. She meets with nothing beyond her demerits, when in the full view of the horrors of which her wickedness has been the guilty cause, with her own hands she strangles herself. It is wisely done that the poet dismisses her from the scene before the final disclosure, that the sympathy of the spectators may not be frittered away and diverted from the more worthy Oedipus.

JOHN WILLIAMS WHITE

1875.

Introductory Note

Sophocles, the most perfectly balanced among the three great masters of Greek tragedy, was born in Colonus, near Athens, about 495 B. C. His father was a man of wealth, and the poet received the best education of the time, being especially distinguished in music. He began his career as a dramatist at the age of twenty-seven, when he gained a victory over Æschylus; and from that time till his death in 405 B. C. he retained the foremost place as a writer of tragedy. Like a true Greek, he played his part in public affairs, both in peace and in war, and served his country as a diplomat and as a general. He was profoundly admired by his contemporaries for character as well as genius, and after his death was honored as a hero with annual sacrifices. His son, Iophon, and his grandson, Sophocles, both gained distinction as tragic poets.

Besides lyrics, elegies, and epigrams, Sophocles is said to have composed upward of one hundred and twenty plays, one hundred of which are known by name, but only seven have come down to us entire. These are the "Trachiniæ," dealing with the death of Heracles; "Ajax," "Philoctetes," "Electra," "Oedipus Rex," "Oedipus at Colonus," and Antigone."

The development of tragedy by Æschylus was continued by Sophocles, who introduced a third actor and, later, a fourth; reduced still further the importance of the chorus, and elaborated the costumes of the players. He did not, like Æschylus, write trilogies which carried one story through three plays, but made each work complete in itself. The art of clear and full characterization was carried to a pitch of perfection by him, the figures in the plays of Æschylus being in comparison rather drawings in outline, while those of Euripides are frequently direct transcripts from real life, without the idealization given by Sophocles. With his restraint, his balance, his clearness of vision, his aptness in the fitting of means to ends, and the beauty of his style, he stands as the most perfect example in literature of the characteristic excellences of the Greek artist. In the two dramas here given will be found illustrations of these qualities at their highest.

DRAMATIS PERSONAE

Oedipus, *King of Thebes*
Creon, *brother of* Jocasta
Teiresias, *a soothsayer*
Priest of Zeus
Messenger from Corinth
Shepherd
Second Messenger
Jocasta, *wife of* Oedipus
Chorus of Priests and Suppliants

SCENE—*Thebes. In the background, the palace of* OEDIPUS; *in front, the altar of* ZEUS, *Priests and Boys round it in the attitude of suppliants.*

OEDIPUS REX

[*Enter* OEDIPUS.]

OEDIPUS. WHY sit ye here, my children, brood last reared
    Of Cadmus famed of old, in solemn state,
    Uplifting in your hands the suppliants' boughs?
    And all the city reeks with incense smoke,
    And all re-echoes with your wailing hymns;
    And I, my children, counting it unmeet
    To hear report from others, I have come
    Myself, whom all name Oedipus the Great.—
    Do thou, then, agèd Sire, since thine the right
    To speak for these, tell clearly why ye stand   10
    Awe-stricken, or adoring; speak to me
    As willing helper. Dull and cold this heart
    To see you prostrate thus, and feel no ruth.
PRIEST. Yes, Oedipus, thou ruler of my land,
    Thou seest us how we sit, as suppliants, bowed
    Around thine altars; some as yet unfledged
    To wing their flight, and some weighed down with age.
    Priest, I, of Zeus, and these the chosen youth:
    And in the open spaces of the town
    The people sit and wail, with wreath in hand,   20
    By the twin shrine of Pallas,[1] or the grove
    Oracular that bears Ismenus' name.
    For this our city, as thine eyes may see,
    Is sorely tempest-tossed, nor lifts its head
    From out the surging sea of blood-flecked waves,
    All smitten in the fruitful blooms of earth,
    All smitten in the herds that graze the fields,
    Yea, and in timeless births of woman's fruit;
    And still the God sends forth his darts of fire,
    And lays us low. The plague, abhorred and feared,   30
    Makes desolate the home where Cadmus dwelt,
    And Hades dark grows rich in sighs and groans.
    It is not that we count thee as a God,
    Equalled with them in power, that we sit here,
    These little ones and I, as suppliants prone;
    But, judging thee, in all life's shifting scenes,

---

[1] Probably, as at Athens Athena had two temples as Polias and Parthenos, so also at Thebes there were two shrines dedicated to her under different names, as Onkæa and Ismenia.

Chiefest of men, yea, and of chiefest skill,
To soothe the powers of Heaven. For thou it was
That freed this city, named of Cadmus old,
From the sad tribute which of yore we paid   40
To that stern songstress,[2] all untaught of us,
And all unprompted; but at God's behest,
Men think and say, thou guidest all our life.
And now, O Oedipus, most honoured lord,
We pray thee, we, thy suppliants, find for us
Some succour, whether floating voice of God,
Or speech of man brings knowledge to thy soul;
For still I see, with those whom life has trained
To long-tried skill, the issues of their thoughts
Live and are mighty. Come, then, noblest one,   50
Come, save our city; look on us, and fear.
As yet this land, for all thy former zeal,
Calls thee its saviour: do not give us cause
So to remember this thy reign, as men
Who, having risen, then fall low again;
But save us, save our city. Omens good
Were then with thee; thou didst thy work, and now
Be equal to thyself! If thou wilt rule,
As thou dost rule, this land wherein we dwell,
'Twere better far to reign o'er living men   60
Than o'er a realm dispeopled. Naught avails,
Or tower or ship, when crew and guards are gone.
OEDIPUS. O children, wailing loud, ye tell me not
Of woes unknown; too well I know them all,
Your sorrows and your wants. For one and all
Are stricken, yet no sorrow like to mine
Weighs on you. Each his own sad burden bears,
His own and not another's. But my heart
Mourns for the people's sorrow and mine own;
And, lo! ye have not come to break my sleep,   70
But found me weeping, weeping bitter tears,
And treading weary paths in wandering thought;
And that one way of healing which I found,
That have I acted on. Menœkeus' son,
Creon, my kinsman, have I sent to seek
The Pythian home of Phœbus, there to learn
The words or deeds wherewith to save the state;
And even now I measure o'er the time

---

[2] The tribute of human victims paid to the Sphinx, the "Muse of the slaughtered," till her riddle was solved by Oedipus.

And wonder how he fares, for, lo! he stays,
I know not why, beyond the appointed day;   80
But when he comes I should be base indeed,
Failing to do whate'er the God declares.
PRIEST. Well hast thou spoken! Tidings come e'en now
    Of Creon seen approaching.
OEDIPUS. Grant, O King
    Apollo, that he come with omen good,
    Bright with the cheer of one that bringeth life.
PRIEST. If one may guess, 'tis well. He had not come
    His head all wreathed[3] with boughs of laurel else.
OEDIPUS. Soon we shall know. Our voice can reach him now.   90
    Say, prince, our well-beloved, Menœkeus' son,
    What sacred answer bring'st thou from the God?

[*Enter* CREON]

CREON. A right good answer! That our evil plight,
    If all goes well, may end in highest good.
OEDIPUS. What means this speech? Nor full of eager hope,
    Nor trembling panic, list I to thy words.
CREON. I for my part am ready, these being by,
    To tell thee all, or go within the gates.
OEDIPUS. Speak out to all. I sorrow more for them
    Than for the woe which touches me alone.   100
CREON. Well, then, I speak the things the God declared.
    Phœbus, our king, he bids us chase away
    (The words were plain) the infection of our land,
    Nor cherish guilt which still remains unhealed.
OEDIPUS. But with what rites? And what the deed itself?
CREON. Drive into exile, blood for blood repay.
    That guilt of blood is blasting all the state.
OEDIPUS. But whose fate is it that thou hintest at?
CREON. Once, O my king, ere thou didst raise our state,
    Our sovereign Laius ruled o'er all the land.   110
OEDIPUS. This know I well, though him I never saw.
CREON. Well, then, the God commands us, he being dead,
    To take revenge on those who shed his blood.
OEDIPUS. Yes; but where are they? How to track the course
    Of guilt all shrouded in the doubtful past?
CREON. In this our land, so said he, those who seek
    Shall find; unsought, we lose it utterly.

---

[3] Creon, coming from Delphi, wears a wreath of the Parnassian laurel, its red berries mingling with the dark, glossy leaves.

OEDIPUS. Was it at home, or in the field, or else
   In some strange land that Laius met his doom?
CREON. He went, so spake he, pilgrim-wise afar,   120
   And nevermore came back as forth he went.
OEDIPUS. Was there no courier, none who shared his road,
   From whom, inquiring, one might learn the truth?
CREON. Dead are they all, save one who fled for fear,
   And he had naught to tell but this;...
OEDIPUS. [*Interrupting*] And what was that? One fact might teach us
      much,
   Had we but one small starting-point of hope.
CREON. He used to tell that robbers fell on him,
   Not man for man, but with outnumbering force.
OEDIPUS. Yet sure no robber would have dared this deed,   130
   Unless some bribe had tempted him from hence.
CREON. So men might think; but Laius at his death
   Found none to help, or 'venge him in his woe.
OEDIPUS. What hindered you, when thus your sovereignty
   Had fallen low, from searching out the truth?
CREON. The Sphinx, with her dark riddle, bade us look
   At nearer facts, and leave the dim obscure.
OEDIPUS. Well, be it mine to track them to their source.
   Right well hath Phœbus, and right well hast thou,
   Shown for the dead your care, and ye shall find,   140
   As is most meet, in me a helper true,
   Aiding at once my country and the God.
   Not for the sake of friends, or near or far,
   But for mine own, will I dispel this curse;
   For he that slew him, whosoe'er he be,
   Will wish, perchance, with such a blow to smite
   Me also. Helping him, I help myself.
   And now, my children, rise with utmost speed
   From off these steps, and raise your suppliant boughs;
   And let another call my people here,   150
   The race of Cadmus, and make known that I
   Will do my taskwork to the uttermost:
   So, as God wills, we prosper, or we fail.
PRIEST. Rise, then, my children, 'twas for this we came,
   For these good tidings which those lips have brought,
   And Phœbus, he who sent these oracles,
   Pray that he come to heal, and save from woe.

   [*Exeunt* CREON *and Priest.*]

STROPHE I

CHORUS. O voice of Zeus[4] sweet-toned, with what intent
　　Cam'st thou from Pytho, where the red gold shines,
　　To Thebes, of high estate?　　　　　　　　　　160
　　Fainting for fear, I quiver in suspense
　　(Hear us, O healer! God of Delos,[5] hear!),
　　In brooding dread, what doom, of present growth,
　　Or as the months roll on, thy hand will work;
　　Tell me, O Voice divine, thou child of golden hope!

ANTISTROPHE I

　　Thee first, Zeus-born Athene, thee I call;
　　And next thy sister, Goddess of our land,
　　Our Artemis, who in the market sits
　　In queenly pride, upon her orbed throne;
　　And Phœbus, the fair darter! O ye Three,[6]　　170
　　Shine on us, and deliver us from ill!
　　If e'er before, when waves or storms of woe
　　Rushed on our state, ye drove away
　　The fiery tide of ill,
　　Come also now!

STROPHE II

　　Yea, come, ye Gods, for sorrows numberless
　　　　Press on my soul;
　　And all the host is smitten, and our thoughts
　　　　Lack weapons to resist.
　　For increase fails of all the fruits of earth,　　180
　　And women faint in childbirth's wailing pangs,
　　And one by one, as flit the swift-winged birds,
　　So, flitting to the shore of Hades dark,[7]
　　Fleeter than lightning's flash,
　　Thou seest them passing on.

---

[4] The oracle, though given by Apollo, is yet the voice of Zeus, of whom Apollo is but the prophet, spokesman.

[5] Apollo, born in Delos, passed through Attica to Pytho, his shrine at Delphi.

[6] The Three named—Athena, Artemis, Phœbos—were the guardian deities of Thebes; but the tendency to bring three names together in one group in oaths and invocations runs through Greek worship generally.

[7] Pluto, dwelling where the sun sinks into darkness. The symbolism of the West as the region of dead and evil, of the East as that of light and truth, belongs to the earliest parables of nature.

ANTISTROPHE II

Yea, numberless are they who perish thus,
And on the soil, plague-breeding, lie
Infants unpitied, cast out ruthlessly;
And wives and mothers, gray with hoary age,
Some here, some there, by every altar mourn,   190
With woe and sorrow crushed,
And chant their wailing plaint.
Clear thrills the sense their solemn litany,
And the low anthem sung in unison.
Hear, then, thou golden daughter of great Zeus,
And send us help, bright-faced as is the morn.

STROPHE III

And Ares the destroyer drive away![8]
Who now, though hushed the din of brazen shield,
With battle-cry wars on me fierce and hot.
Bid him go back in flight,   200
Retreat from this our land,
Or to the ocean bed,
Where Amphitrite sleeps,
Or to the homeless sea
Which sweeps the Thracian shore.[9]
If waning night spares aught
That doth the day assail:
Do thou, then, Sire almighty,
Wielding the lightning's strength,
Blast him with thy hot thunder.   210

ANTISTROPHE III

And thou, Lyceian king, the wolf's dread foe,
Fain would I see thy darts
From out thy golden bow
Go forth invincible,
Helping and bringing aid;

---

[8] The Pestilence, previously (v. 27) personified, is now identified with Ares, the God of slaughter, and, as such, the foe of the more benign deities.

[9] The Chorus prays that the pestilence may be driven either to the far western ocean, beyond the pillars of Heracles, the couch of Amphitrite, the bride of Neptune, or to the northern coasts of the Euxine, where Ares was worshipped as the special God of the Thracians.

And with them, winged with fire,
The rays of Artemis,
With which, on Lycian hills,
She moveth on her course.
And last I call on thee,   220
Thou of the golden crown,
Guardian of this our land,[10]
Bacchus, all purple-flushed,
With clamour loud and long,
Wandering with Maenads wild;
I call on thee to come,
Flashing with blazing torch,
Against the God whom all the Gods disown.[11]

OEDIPUS. Thou prayest, and for thy prayers, if thou wilt hear
My words, and treat the dire disease with skill,   230
Thou shalt find help and respite from thy pain,—
My words, which I, a stranger to report,
A stranger to the deed, will now declare:
For I myself should fail to track it far,
Unless some footprints guided me aright.
But now, since here I stand, the latest come,
A citizen to citizens, I speak
To all the sons of Cadmus. Lives there one
Who knows of Laius, son of Labdacus,
The hand that slew him; him I bid to tell   240
His tale to me; and should it chance he shrinks,
Fearing the charge against himself to bring,
Still let him speak; no heavier doom is his
Than to depart uninjured from the land;
Or, if there be that knows an alien arm
As guilty, let him hold his peace no more;
I will secure his gain and thanks beside.
But if ye hold your peace, if one through fear
Shall stifle words his bosom friend may drop,
What then I purpose let him hear from me: 250
That man I banish, whosoe'er he be,
From out the land whose power and throne are mine;
And none may give him shelter, none speak to him,
Nor join with him in prayer and sacrifice,
Nor pour for him the stream that cleanses guilt;
But all shall thrust him from their homes, abhorred,

---

[10] Bacchos, as born in Thebes, was known as the Cadmeian king, the Boeotian God, while Thebes took from him the epithet Bacchia.

[11] So, in the Iliad, Ares is, of all the Gods of Olympos, most hateful to Zeus (v. 890), as the cause of all strife and slaughter.

Our curse and our pollution, as the word
Prophetic of the Pythian God has shown:
Such as I am, I stand before you here,
A helper to the God and to the dead.   260
And for the man who did the guilty deed,
Whether alone he lurks, or leagued with more,
I pray that he may waste his life away,
For vile deeds vilely dying; and for me,
If in my house, I knowing it, he dwells,
May every curse I speak on my head fall.
And this I charge you do, for mine own sake,[12]
And for the God's, and for the land that pines,
Barren and god-deserted. Wrong 'twould be,
E'en if no voice from heaven had urged us on,   270
That ye should leave the stain of guilt uncleansed,
Your noblest chief, your king himself, being slain.
Yea, rather, seek and find. And since I reign,
Wielding the might his hand did wield before,
Filling his couch, and calling his wife mine,
Yea, and our children too, but for the fate
That fell on his, had grown up owned by both;
But so it is. On his head fell the doom;
And therefore will I strive my best for him,
As for my father, and will go all lengths   280
To seek and find the murderer, him who slew
The son of Labdacus, and Polydore,
And earlier Cadmus, and Agenor old;[13]
And for all those who hearken not, I pray
The Gods to give then neither fruit of earth,
Nor seed of woman,[14] but consume their lives
With this dire plague, or evil worse than this.
And you, the rest, the men from Cadmus sprung,
To whom these words approve themselves as good,
May righteousness befriend you, and the Gods,   290
In full accord, dwell with you evermore.
CHORUS. Since thou hast bound me by a curse, O king,
I needs must speak. I neither slew the man,
Nor know who slew. To say who did the deed
Belongs to him who sent this oracle.
OEDIPUS. Right well thou speak'st, but man's best strength must fail

---

[12] I follow Schneidewin's arrangement of this portion of the speech.

[13] Oedipus, as if identifying himself already with the kingly house, goes through the whole genealogy up to the remote ancestor.

[14] The imprecation agrees almost verbally with the curse of the Amphictyonic councils against sacrilege.

To force the Gods to do the things they will not.
CHORUS. And may I speak a second time my thoughts?
OEDIPUS. If 'twere a third, shrink not from speaking out.
CHORUS. One man I know, a prince, whose insight deep   300
    Sees clear as princely Phœbus, and from him,
    Teiresias, one might learn, O king, the truth.
OEDIPUS. That, too, is done. No loiterer I in this,
    For I have sent, on Creon's hint, two bands
    To summon him, and wonder that he comes not.
CHORUS. Old rumours are there also, dark and dumb.
OEDIPUS. And what are they? I weigh the slightest word.
CHORUS. 'Twas said he died by some chance traveller's hand.
OEDIPUS. I, too, heard that. But none knows who was by.
CHORUS. If yet his soul is capable of awe,   310
    Hearing thy curses, he will shrink from them.
OEDIPUS. Words fright not him who, doing, knows no fear.
CHORUS. Well, here is one who'll put him to the proof.
    For, lo! they bring the seer inspired of God;
    Chosen of all men, vessel of the truth.

[*Enter* TEIRESIAS, *blind, and guided by a boy.*]

OEDIPUS. Teiresias! thou whose mind embraceth all,
    Told or untold, the things of heaven or earth;
    Thou knowest, although thou seest not, what a pest
    Dwells on us, and we find in thee, O prince,
    Our one deliverer, yea, our only help.   320
    For Phœbus (if, perchance, thou hast not heard)
    Sent back this word to us, who sent to ask,
    That this one way was open to escape
    From the fell plague; if those who Laius slew,
    We in our turn, discovering, should slay,
    Or drive them forth as exiles from the land.
    Thou, therefore, grudge not either sign from birds,
    Or any other path of prophecy;
    But save the city, save thyself, save me;
    Lift off the guilt that death has left behind;   330
    On thee we hang. To use our means, our power,
    In doing good, is noblest service owned.
TEIRESIAS. Ah me! ah me! how sad is wisdom's gift,
    When no good issue waiteth on the wise!
    Right well I knew this, but in evil hour
    Forgot, alas! or else I had not come.
OEDIPUS. What means this? How despondingly thou com'st!
TEIRESIAS. Let me go home; for thus thy fate shalt thou,

And I mine own, bear easiest, if thou yield.
OEDIPUS. No loyal words thou speak'st, nor true to Thebes   340
    Who reared thee, holding back this oracle.
TEIRESIAS. It is because I see thy lips speak words
    Ill-timed, ill-omened, that I guard my speech.
OEDIPUS. Now, by the Gods, unless thy reason fails,
    Refuse us not, who all implore thy help.
TEIRESIAS. Yes. Reason fails you all; but ne'er will I
    So speak my sorrows as to unveil thine.
OEDIPUS. What mean'st thou, then? Thou know'st and wilt not tell,
    But giv'st to ruin both the state and us?
TEIRESIAS. I will not pain myself nor thee. Why, then,   350
    All vainly urge it? Thou shalt never know.
OEDIPUS. Oh, basest of the base! (for thou wouldst stir
    A heart of stone;) and wilt thou never tell,
    But still abide relentless and unmoved?
TEIRESIAS. My mood thou blamest, but thou dost not know
    That which dwells with thee while thou chidest me.
OEDIPUS. And who would not feel anger, as he hears
    The words which bring dishonour to the state?
TEIRESIAS. Well! come they will, though I should hold my
        peace.
OEDIPUS. If come they must, thy duty is to speak.   360
TEIRESIAS. I speak no more. So, if thou wilt, rage on,
    With every mood of wrath most desperate.
OEDIPUS. Yes; I will not refrain, so fierce my wrath,
    From speaking all my thought. I think that thou
    Didst plot the deed, and do it, though the blow
    Thy hands, it may be, dealt not. Hadst thou seen,
    I would have said it was thy deed alone
TEIRESIAS. And it has come to this? I charge thee, hold
    To thy late edict, and from this day forth
    Speak not to me, nor yet to these, for thou,   370
    Thou art the accursèd plague-spot of the land.
OEDIPUS. Art thou so shameless as to vent such words,
    And thinkest to escape thy righteous doom?
TEIRESIAS. I have escaped. The strength of truth is mine.
OEDIPUS. Who prompted thee? This comes not from thine art.
TEIRESIAS. Thou art the man. 'Twas thou who mad'st me speak.
OEDIPUS. What say'st thou? Tell it yet again, that I
    May know more clearly.
TEIRESIAS. When I spoke before,
    Didst thou not know? Or dost thou challenge me?   380
OEDIPUS. I could not say I knew it. Speak again.
TEIRESIAS. I say that thou stand'st there a murderer.

OEDIPUS. Thou shalt not twice revile, and go unharmed.
TEIRESIAS. And shall I tell thee more to stir thy rage?
OEDIPUS. Say what thou pleasest. All in vain 'tis said.
TEIRESIAS. I say that thou, in vilest intercourse
    With those thou lovest best, dost blindly live,
    Nor seest the evil thou hast made thine own.
OEDIPUS. And dost thou think to say these things and live?
TEIRESIAS. Of that I doubt not, if truth holds her own.   390
OEDIPUS. Truth is for all but thee, but thou hast none,
    Blind in thine ears, thy reason, and thine eyes.
TEIRESIAS. How wretched thou, thus hurling this reproach!
    Such, all too soon, the world will hurl at thee.
OEDIPUS. Thou livest wrapt in one continual night,
    And canst not hurt or me, or any man
    Who sees the light.
TEIRESIAS. Fate's firm decree stands fixed:
    Thou diest not by me. Apollo's might
    Suffices. His the task to bring thee low.   400
OEDIPUS. Are these devices Creon's or thine own?
TEIRESIAS. It is not Creon harms thee, but thyself.
OEDIPUS. O wealth, and sovereignty, and noblest skill
    Surpassing skill in life that men admire,
    How great the envy dogging all your steps!
    If for the sake of kingship, which the state
    Hath given, unasked for, freely in mine hands,
    Creon the faithful, found mine earliest friend,
    Now seeks with masked attack to drive me forth,
    And hires this wizard, plotter of foul schemes,   410
    A vagrant mountebank, whose sight is clear
    For pay alone, but in his art stone-blind.
    Is it not so? When wast thou known a seer?
    Why, when the monster with her song was here,
    Didst thou not give our countrymen thy help?
    And yet the riddle lay above the ken
    Of common men, and called for prophet's skill.
    And this thou show'dst thou hadst not, nor by bird,
    Nor any God made known; but then I came,
    I, Oedipus, who nothing knew, and slew her,   420
    With mine own counsel winning, all untaught
    By flight of birds. And now thou wouldst expel me,
    And think'st to take thy stand by Creon's throne.
    But, as I think, both thou and he that plans
    With thee, will to your cost attack my fame;
    And but that thou stand'st there all old and weak,
    Thou shouldst be taught what kind of plans are thine.

CHORUS. Far as we dare to measure, both his words
    And thine, O Oedipus, in wrath are said.
    Not such as these we need, but this to see,   430
    How best to do the bidding of the God.
TEIRESIAS. King though thou be, I claim an equal right
    To make reply. Here I call no man lord:
    For I am not thy slave, but Loxias';[15]
    Nor shall I stand on Creon's patronage;
    And this I say, since thou hast dared revile
    My blindness, that thou seest, yet dost not see
    Thy evil plight, nor where thou liv'st, nor yet
    With whom thou dwellest, Know'st thou even this,
    Whence thou art sprung? All ignorant thou sinn'st   440
    Against thine own, the living and the dead.
    And soon a curse from mother and from sire
    With fearful foot shall chase thee forth from us,
    Now seeing all things clear, then all things dark.
    And will not then each shore repeat thy wail,
    And will not old Kithæron echoing ring
    When thou discern'st the marriage, fatal port,
    To which thy prosp'rous voyage brought thy bark?
    And other ills, in countless multitude,
    Thou seest not yet, on thee and on thy seed   450
    Shall fall alike. Vent forth thy wrath then loud,
    On Creon and on me. There lives not man
    Who wastes his life more wretchedly than thou.
OEDIPUS. This can be borne no longer! Out with thee!
    A curse light on thee! Wilt thou not depart?
    Wilt thou not turn and wend thy backward way?
TEIRESIAS. I had not come hadst thou not called me here.
OEDIPUS. I knew not thou wouldst speak so foolishly;
    Else I had hardly fetched thee to my house.
TEIRESIAS. We then, for thee (so deemest thou), are fools,   460
    But, for thy parents, who begot thee, wise. [*Turns to go.*]
OEDIPUS. [*Starting forward.*] What? Stay thy foot. What mortal gave
    me birth?
TEIRESIAS. This day shall give thy birth, and work thy doom.
OEDIPUS. What riddles dark and dim thou lov'st to speak.
TEIRESIAS. Yes. But thy skill excels in solving such.
OEDIPUS. Scoff as thou wilt, in this thou'lt find me strong.
TEIRESIAS. And yet success in this has worked thy fall.
OEDIPUS. I little care, if I have saved the state.

---

[15] The special name of Apollo as the *prophetes* of Zeus, and therefore the guardian of all seers and prophets.

TEIRESIAS. Well, then, I go. Do thou, boy, lead me on!
OEDIPUS. Let him lead on. So hateful art thou near,   470
   Thou canst not pain me more when thou art gone.
TEIRESIAS. I go, then, having said the things I came
   To say. No fear of thee compels me. Thine
   Is not the power to hurt me. And I say,
   This man whom thou art seeking out with threats,
   As murderer of Laius, he is here,
   In show an alien sojourner, but in truth
   A home-born Theban. No delight to him
   Will that discovery bring. Blind, having seen,
   Poor, having rolled in wealth,—he, with a staff   480
   Feeling his way, to other lands shall go!
   And by his sons shall he be known at once
   Father and brother, and of her who bore him
   Husband and son, sharing his father's bed,
   His father's murd'rer. Go thou, then, within,
   And brood o'er this, and, if thou find'st me fail,
   Say that my skill in prophecy is gone.

[*Exeunt* OEDIPUS *and* TEIRESIAS.]

STROPHE I

CHORUS. Who was it that the rock oracular
    Of Delphi spake of, working
With bloody hand his nameless deed of shame?   490
     Time is it now for him,
     Swifter than fastest steed,
     To bend his course in flight.
     For, in full armour clad,
     Upon him darts, with fire
And lightning flash, the radiant Son of Zeus.
And with him come in train the dreaded ones,
    The Destinies that may not be appeased.

ANTISTROPHE I

For from Parnassus' heights, enwreathed with snow,
Gleaming, but now there shone   500
The oracle that bade us, one and all,
   Track the unnamed, unknown one.
For, lo! he wanders through the forest wild,
    In caves and over rocks,
    As strays the mountain bull,

In dreary loneliness with dreary tread,
    Seeking in vain to shun
The words prophetic of the central shrine;[16]
Yet they around him hover, full of life.

STROPHE II

Dread things, yea, dread, the augur skilled has stirred   510
That leave the question open, aye or no!
And which to say I know not,
But hover still in hopes, and fail to scan
Things present or to come.
For neither now nor in the former years
Learnt I what cause of strife
Set the Labdacid race
At variance with the house of Polybus.
Nor can I test the tale,
And take my stand against the well-earned fame   520
    Of Oedipus, my lord,
As champion of the house of Labdacus,
    For deaths that none may trace!

ANTISTROPHE II

For Zeus and King Apollo, they are wise,
    And know the hearts of men:
But that a prophet passeth me in skill,
    This is no judgment true;
And one man may another's wisdom pass,
    By wisdom higher still.
I, for my part, before the word is clear,   530
Will ne'er assent to those that speak in blame.
'Tis clear, the Maiden-monster with her wings
Came on him, and he proved by sharpest test
That he was wise, by all the land beloved,
And, from my heart at least,
The charge of baseness comes not.

[*Enter* CREON]

---

[16] Delphi, thought of by the Greeks, as Jerusalem was in the middle ages, as the centre of the whole earth.

CREON. I come, my friends, as having learnt but now
    Our ruler, Oedipus, accuses me
    With dreadful words I cannot bear to hear.
    For if, in these calamities of ours,   540
    He thinks he suffers wrongly at my hands,
    In word or deed, aught tending to his hurt,
    I set no value on a life prolonged,
    If this reproach hangs on me; for its harm
    Affects not slightly, but is direst shame,
    If through the land my name as villain rings,
    By thee and by thy friends a villain called.
CHORUS. But this reproach, it may be, came from wrath
    All hasty, rather than from judgment calm.
CREON. And who informed him that the seer, seduced   550
    By my false counsel, spoke his lying words?
CHORUS. The words were said, but on what grounds I know not.
CREON. And was it with calm eyes and judgment clear,
    The charge was brought against my name and fame?
CHORUS. I cannot say. To what our rulers do
    I close my eyes. But here he comes himself.

    [*Enter* OEDIPUS]

OEDIPUS. Ho, there! is't thou? And does thy boldness soar
    So shameless as to come beneath my roof,
    When thou, 'tis clear, hast done the deed of blood,
    And now wilt rob me of my sovereignty?   560
    Is it, by all the Gods, that thou hast seen
    Or cowardice or folly in my soul,
    That thou hast laid thy plans? Or thoughtest thou
    That I should neither see thy sinuous wiles,
    Nor, knowing, ward them off? This scheme of thine,
    Is it not wild, backed nor by force nor friends,
    To seek the power which calls for force or wealth?
CREON. Do as thou pleasest. But for words of scorn
    Hear like words back, and as thou hearest, judge.
OEDIPUS. Cunning of speech art thou! But I am slow   570
    To learn of thee, whom I have found my foe.
CREON. Hear this, then, first, that thus I have to speak....
OEDIPUS. But this, then, say not, that thou art not vile.
CREON. If that thou thinkest self-willed pride avails,
    Apart from judgment, know thou art not wise.
OEDIPUS. If that thou thinkest, injuring thy friend,
    To do it unchastised, thou art not wise.

CREON. In this, I grant, thou speakest right; but tell,
  What form of suffering hast thou to endure?
OEDIPUS. Didst thou, or didst thou not, thy counsel give   580
  Some one to send to fetch this reverend seer?
CREON. And even now by that advice I hold!
OEDIPUS. How long a time has passed since Laius chanced...
  [*Pauses.*]
CREON. Chanced to do what? I understand not yet.
OEDIPUS. Since he was smitten with the deadly blow?
CREON. The years would measure out a long, long tale.
OEDIPUS. And was this seer then practising his art?
CREON. Full wise as now, and equal in repute.
OEDIPUS. Did he at that time say a word of me?
CREON. No word, while I, at any rate, was by.   590
OEDIPUS. And yet ye held your quest upon the dead?
CREON. Of course we held it, but we nothing heard.
OEDIPUS. How was it he, the wise one, spoke not then?
CREON. I know not, and, not knowing, hold my peace.
OEDIPUS. One thing thou know'st, and, meaning well, wouldst speak!
CREON. And what is that? for if I know, I'll speak.
OEDIPUS. Why, unless thou wert in the secret, then
  He spake not of me as the murderer.
CREON. If he says this, thou know'st it. I of thee
  Desire to learn, as thou hast learnt of me.   600
OEDIPUS. Learn then; no guilt of blood shall rest on me.
CREON. Well, then,—my sister? dost thou own her wife?
OEDIPUS. I will not meet this question with denial.
CREON. And sharest thou an equal rule with her?
OEDIPUS. Her every wish by me is brought to act.
CREON. And am not I co-equal with you twain?
OEDIPUS. Yes; and just here thou show'st thyself false friend.
CREON. Not so, if thou wouldst reason with thyself,
  As I must reason. First reflect on this:
  Supposest thou that one would rather choose   610
  To reign with fears than sleeping calmest sleep,
  His power being equal? I, for one, prize less
  The name of king than deeds of kingly power;
  And so would all who learn in wisdom's school.
  Now without fear I have what I desire,
  At thy hand given. Did I rule, myself,
  I might do much unwillingly. Why, then,
  Should sovereignty exert a softer charm
  Than power and might unchequered by a care?
  I am not yet so cheated by myself   620
  As to desire aught else but honest gain.

Now all goes well, now every one salutes,
Now they who seek thy favour court my smiles,
For on this hinge does all their fortune turn.
Why, then, should I leave this to hunt for that?
My mind, retaining reason, ne'er could act
The villain's part. I was not born to love
Such thoughts myself, nor bear with those that do.
And as a proof of this, go thou thyself,
And ask at Pytho whether I brought back,   630
In very deed, the oracles I heard.
And if thou find me plotting with the seer,
In common concert, not by one decree,
But two, thine own and mine, proclaim my death.
But charge me not with crime on shadowy proof;
For neither is it just, in random thought,
The bad to count as good, nor good as bad;
For to thrust out a friend of noble heart,
Is like the parting with the life we love.
And this in time thou'lt know, for time alone   640
Makes manifest the righteous. Of the vile
Thou mayst detect the vileness in a day.
CHORUS. To one who fears to fall, he speaketh well;
    O king, swift counsels are not always safe.
OEDIPUS. But when a man is swift in wily schemes,
    Swift must I be to baffle plot with plot;
    And if I stand and wait, he wins the day,
    And all my life is found one great mistake.
CREON. What seek'st thou, then? to drive me from the land?
OEDIPUS. Not so. I seek not banishment, but death.   650
CREON. When thou show'st first what grudge I bear to thee?
OEDIPUS. And say'st thou this defying, yielding not?
CREON. I see thy judgment fails.
OEDIPUS. I hold mine own.
CREON. Mine has an equal claim.
OEDIPUS. Thou villain born!
CREON. And if thy mind is darkened…?
OEDIPUS. Still obey!
CREON. Not to a tyrant ruler.
OEDIPUS. O my country!   660
CREON. I, too, can claim that country. 'Tis not thine!
CHORUS. Cease, O my princes! In good time I see
    Jocasta coming hither from the house;
    And it were well with her to hush this strife.

[*Enter* JOCASTA]

JOCASTA. Why, O ye wretched ones, this strife of tongues
    Raise ye in your unwisdom, nor are shamed,
    Our country suffering, private griefs to stir?
    Come thou within. And thou, O Creon, go,
    Nor bring a trifling sore to mischief great!
CREON. My sister! Oedipus, thy husband, claims   670
    The right to wrong me, giving choice of ills,
    Or to be exiled from my home, or die.
OEDIPUS. 'Tis even so, for I have found him, wife,
    Against my life his evil wiles devising.
CREON. May I ne'er prosper, but accursed die,
    If I have done the things he says I did!
JOCASTA. Oh, by the Gods, believe him, Oedipus!
    Respect his oath, which calls the Gods to hear;
    And reverence me, and these who stand by thee.
CHORUS. Hearken, my king! be calmer, I implore!   680
OEDIPUS. What! wilt thou that I yield?
CHORUS. Respect is due
    To one not weak before, who now is strong
    In this his oath.
OEDIPUS. And know'st thou what thou ask'st?
CHORUS. I know right well.
OEDIPUS. Say on, then, what thou wilt.
CHORUS. Hurl not to shame, on grounds of mere mistrust,
    The friend on whom his own curse still must hang.
OEDIPUS. Know, then, that, seeking this, thou seek'st, in truth,   690
    To work my death, or else my banishment.
CHORUS. Nay, by the sun, chief God of all the Gods![17]
    May I, too, die, of God and man accursed,
    If I wish aught like this! But on my soul,
    Our wasting land dwells heavily; ills on ills
    Still coming, and your strife embittering all.
OEDIPUS. Let him depart, then, even though I die,
    Or from my country wander forth in shame:
    Thy face, not his, I view with pitying eye;
    For him, where'er he be, is naught but hate.   700
CREON. Thou'rt loath to yield, 'twould seem, and wilt be
    vexed
    When this thy wrath is over: moods like thine
    Are fitly to themselves most hard to bear.
OEDIPUS. Wilt thou not go, and leave me?

---

[17] Helios, specially invoked as the giver of light, discerning and making manifest all hidden things.

CREON. I will go,
 By thee misjudged, but known as just by these. [*Exit.*]
CHORUS. Why, lady, art thou slow to lead him in?
JOCASTA. I fain would learn how this sad chance arose.
CHORUS. Blind hasty speech there was, and wrong will sting.
JOCASTA. From both of them?   710
CHORUS. Yea, both.
JOCASTA. And what said each?
CHORUS. Enough for me, our land laid low in grief,
 It seems, to leave the quarrel where it stopped.
OEDIPUS. Seest thou, with all thy purposes of good,
 Thy shifting and thy soothing, what thou dost?
CHORUS. My chief, not once alone I spoke,
 And wild and erring should I be,
 Were I to turn from thee aside,
 Who, when my country rocked in storm,   720
 Righted her course, and, if thou couldst,
 Wouldst send her speeding now.
JOCASTA. Tell me, my king, what cause of fell debate
 Has bred this discord, and provoked thy soul.
OEDIPUS. Thee will I tell, for thee I honour more
 Than these. The cause was Creon and his plots.
JOCASTA. Say, then, if clearly thou canst tell the strife.
OEDIPUS. He says that I am Laius' murderer.
JOCASTA. Of his own knowledge, or by some one taught?
OEDIPUS. Yon scoundrel seer suborning. For himself, 730
 He takes good care to free his lips from blame.
JOCASTA. Leave now thyself, and all thy thoughts of this,
 And list to me, and learn how little skill
 In arts prophetic mortal man may claim;
 And of this truth I'll give thee proof full clear.
 There came to Laius once an oracle
 (I say not that it came from Phœbus' self,
 But from his servants) that his fate was fixed
 By his son's hand to fall—his own and mine:
 And him, so rumour runs, a robber band   740
 Of aliens slew, where meet the three great roads.
 Nor did three days succeed the infant's birth,
 Before, by other hands, he cast him forth,
 Maiming his ankles, on a lonely hill.
 Here, then, Apollo failed to make the boy
 His father's murderer; nor did Laius die
 By his son's hand. So fared the oracles;
 Therefore regard them not. Whate'er the God
 Desires to search he will himself declare.

OEDIPUS. [*Trembling*] O what a fearful boding! thoughts
    disturbed   750
    Thrill through my soul, my queen, at this thy tale.
JOCASTA. What means this shuddering, this averted glance?
OEDIPUS. I thought I heard thee say that Laius died,
    Slain in a skirmish where the three roads meet?
JOCASTA. So was it said, and still the rumours hold.
OEDIPUS. Where was the spot in which this matter passed?
JOCASTA. They call the country Phocis, and the roads.[18]
    From Delphi and from Daulia there converge.
OEDIPUS. And time? what interval has passed since then?
JOCASTA. But just before thou camest to possess   760
    And rule this land the tidings were proclaimed.
OEDIPUS. Great Zeus! what fate hast thou decreed for me?
JOCASTA. What thought is this, my Oedipus, of thine?
OEDIPUS. Ask me not yet, but tell of Laius' frame,
    His build, his features, and his years of life.
JOCASTA. Tall was he, and the white hairs snowed his head,
    And in his face not much unlike to thee.
OEDIPUS. Woe, woe is me! so seems it I have plunged
    All blindly into curses terrible.
JOCASTA. What sayest thou? I shudder as I see thee.   770
OEDIPUS. Desponding fear comes o'er me, lest the seer
    Has seen indeed. But one thing more I'll ask.
JOCASTA. I fear to speak, yet what thou ask'st I'll tell.
OEDIPUS. Went he in humble guise, or with a troop
    Of spearmen, as becomes a man that rules?
JOCASTA. Five were they altogether, and of them
    One was a herald, and one chariot had he.
OEDIPUS. Woe! woe! 'tis all too clear. And who was he
    That told these tidings to thee, O my queen?
JOCASTA. A servant who alone escaped with life.   780
OEDIPUS. And does he chance to dwell among us now?
JOCASTA. Not so; for from the time when he returned,
    And found thee bearing sway, and Laius dead,
    He, at my hand, a suppliant, implored
    This boon, to send him to the distant fields
    To feed his flocks, where never glance of his
    Might Thebes behold. And so I sent him forth;
    For though a slave he might have claimed yet more.
OEDIPUS. And could we fetch him quickly back again?

---

[18] The meeting place of the three roads is now the site of a decayed Turkish village, the *Stavrodrom* of Mparpanas.

    In Æschylos (Fragm. 160), the scene of the murder was laid at Potniæ, on the road between Thebes and Plataea. As the name indicates, the Erinnyes were worshipped there.

JOCASTA. That may well be. But why dost thou wish this?   790
OEDIPUS. I fear, O queen, that words best left unsaid
   Have passed these lips, and therefore wish to see him.
JOCASTA. Well, he shall come. But some small claim have I,
   O king, to learn what touches thee with woe.
OEDIPUS. Thou shalt not fail to learn it, now that I
   Have such forebodings reached. To whom should I
   More than to thee tell all the passing chance?
   I had a father, Polybus of Corinth,
   And Merope of Doris was my mother,
   And I was held in honour by the rest   800
   Who dwelt there, till this accident befel,
   Worthy of wonder, of the heat unworthy
   It roused within me. Thus it chanced: A man
   At supper, in his cups, with wine o'ertaken,
   Reviles me as a spurious changeling boy;
   And I, sore vexed, hardly for that day
   Restrained myself. And when the morrow came
   I went and charged my father and my mother
   With what I thus had heard. They heaped reproach
   On him who stirred the matter, and I soothed   810
   My soul with what they told me; yet it teased,
   Still vexing more and more; and so I went,
   Unknown to them, to Pytho, and the God
   Sent me forth shamed, unanswered in my quest;
   And more he added, dread and dire and dark,
   How that the doom of incest lay on me,
   Most foul, unnatural; and that I should be
   Father of children men would loathe to look on,
   And murderer of the father that begot me.
   And, hearing this, I cast my wistful looks   820
   To where the stars hang over Corinth's towers,
   And fled where nevermore mine eyes might see
   The shame of those dire oracles fulfilled;
   And as I went I reached the spot where he,
   The king, thou tell'st me, met the fatal blow.
   And now, O lady, I will tell thee all.
   Wending my steps that way where three roads meet,
   There met me first a herald, and a man
   Like him thou told'st of, riding on his car,
   Drawn by young colts. With rough and hasty words   830
   They drove me from the road,—the driver first,
   And that old man himself; and then in rage
   I struck the driver, who had turned me back.
   And when the old man saw it, watching me

As by the chariot side I stood, he struck
My forehead with a double-pointed goad.
But we were more than quits, for in a trice
With this right hand I struck him with my staff,
And he rolled backward from his chariot's seat.
And then I slew them all. And if it chance   840
That Laius and this stranger are akin,
What man more wretched than this man who speaks,
What man more harassed by the vexing Gods?
He whom none now, or alien, or of Thebes,
May welcome to their house, or speak to him,
But thrust him forth an exile. And 'twas I,
None other, who against myself proclaimed
These curses. And the bed of him that died
I with my hands, by which he fell, defile.
Am I not vile by nature, all unclean?   850
If I must flee, yet still in flight my doom
Is nevermore to see the friends I love,
Nor tread my country's soil; or else to bear
The guilt of incest, and my father slay,
Yea, Polybus, who reared me from the womb.
Would not a man say right who said that here
Some cruel God was pressing hard on me?
Not that, not that, at least, thou Presence, pure
And awful, of the Gods. May I ne'er look
On such a day as that, but far away   860
Depart unseen from all the haunts of men
Before such great pollution comes on me.
CHORUS. Us, too, O king, these things perplex, yet still,
Till thou hast asked the man who then was by,'
Have hope.
OEDIPUS. And this indeed is all my hope,
Waiting until that shepherd-slave appear.
JOCASTA. And when he comes, what meanest thou to ask?
OEDIPUS. I'll tell thee. Should he now repeat the tale
Thou told'st to me, it frees me from this guilt.   870
JOCASTA. What special word was that thou heard'st from me?
OEDIPUS. Thou said'st he told that robbers slew his lord,
And should he give their number as the same
Now as before, it was not I who slew him,
For one man could not be the same as many.
But if he speak of one man, all alone,
Then, all too plain, the deed cleaves fast to me.
JOCASTA. But know, the thing was said, and clearly said,
And now he cannot from his word draw back.

Not I alone, but the whole city, heard it; 880
And should he now retract his former tale,
Not then, my husband, will he rightly show
The death of Laius, who, as Loxias told,
By my son's hand should die; and yet, poor boy,
He killed him not, but perished long ago.
So I for one, both now and evermore,
Will count all oracles as things of naught.
OEDIPUS. Thou reasonest well. Yet send a messenger
To fetch that peasant. Be not slack in this.
JOCASTA. I will make haste to send. But go thou in; 890
I would do nothing that displeaseth thee. [*Exeunt.*]

STROPHE I

CHORUS. O that my fate were fixed
To live in holy purity of speech,
Pure in all deeds whose laws stand firm and high,
In heaven's clear æther born,
Of whom Olympus only is the sire,
Whom man's frail flesh begat not,
Nor ever shall forgetfulness o'erwhelm;
In them our God is great and grows not old.

ANTISTROPHE I

But pride begets the mood of tyrant power; 900
Pride filled with many thoughts, yet filled in vain,
Untimely, ill-advised,
Scaling the topmost height,
Falls down the steep abyss,
Down to the pit, where step that profiteth
It seeks in vain to take.
I cannot ask the Gods to stop midway
The conflict sore that works our country's good;
I cannot cease to call on God for aid.

STROPHE II

But if there be who walketh haughtily, 910
In action or in speech,
Whom righteousness herself has ceased to awe,
Who counts the temples of the Gods profane,
An evil fate be his,
Fit meed for all his boastfulness of heart;

Unless in time to come he gain his gains
All justly, and draws back from godless deeds,
Nor lays rash hand upon the holy things,
    By man inviolable.
If such deeds prosper who will henceforth pray   920
To guard his soul from passion's fiery darts?
If such as these are held in high repute,
What profit is there of my choral strain?

ANTISTROPHE II

No longer will I go in pilgrim guise,
To yon all holy place, Earth's central shrine,
Nor unto Abae's temple,
Nor to far-famed Olympia,[19]
Unless these pointings of a hand divine
In sight of all men stand out clear and true.
But, O thou sovereign ruler! if that name,   930
O Zeus, belongs to thee, who reign'st o'er all,
Let not this trespass hide itself from thee,
    Or thine undying sway;
    For now they set at naught
    The oracles, half dead,
    That Laius heard of old,
And king Apollo's wonted worship flags,
    And all to wreck is gone
    The homage due to God.

[*Enter* JOCASTA, *followed by an Attendant.*]

JOCASTA. Princes of this our land, across my soul   940
    There comes the thought to go from shrine to shrine
Of all the Gods, these garlands in my hand,
And waving incense; for our Oedipus
Vexes his soul too wildly with his woes,
And speaks not as a man should speak who scans
The present by the experience of the past,
But hangs on every breath that tells of fear.
And since I find that my advice avails not,
To thee, Lyceian King, Apollo, first
I come,—for thou art nearest,—suppliant   950

---

[19] The central shrine is, as in 480, Delphi, where a white oval stone was supposed to be the very centre, or *omphalos* of the earth. At Abæ, in Phocis, was an oracle of Apollo, believed to be older than that of Delphi. In Olympia, the priests of Zeus divined from the clearness or dimness of the fire upon the altar.

With these devotions, trusting thou wilt work
Some way of healing for us, free from guilt;
For now we shudder, all of us, seeing him,
The good ship's pilot, panic-struck and lost.

[*Enter* MESSENGER]

MESSENGER. May I inquire of you, O strangers, where
    To find the house of Oedipus the king,
    And, above all, where he is, if ye know?
CHORUS. This is the house, and he, good sir, within,
    And this his wife, and mother of his children.
MESSENGER. Good fortune be with her and all her kin,   960
    Being, as she is, his true and honoured wife.
JOCASTA. Like fortune be with thee, my friend. Thy speech,
    So kind, deserves no less. But tell me why
    Thou comest, what thou hast to ask or tell.
MESSENGER. Good news to thee, and to thy husband, lady.
JOCASTA. What is it, then? and who has sent thee here?
MESSENGER. I come from Corinth, and the news I'll tell
    May give thee joy. Why not? Yet thou mayst grieve.
JOCASTA. What is the news that has this twofold power?
MESSENGER. The citizens that on these Isthmus dwell   970
    Will make him sovereign. So the rumour ran.
JOCASTA. What then? Is aged Polybus no more?
MESSENGER. E'en so. Death holds him in the stately tomb.
JOCASTA. What say'st thou? Polybus, thy king, is dead?
MESSENGER. If I speak false, I have no wish to live!
JOCASTA. Go, maiden, at thy topmost speed, and tell
    Thy master this. Now, oracles of Gods,
    Where are ye now? Long since my Oedipus
    Fled, fearing lest his hand should slay the man;
    And now he dies by fate, and not by him.   980

[*Enter* OEDIPUS]

OEDIPUS. Mine own Jocasta, why, O dearest one,
    Why hast thou sent to fetch me from the house?
JOCASTA. List this man's tale, and when thou hearest, see
    The woeful plight of those dread oracles.
OEDIPUS. Who, then, is this, and what has he to tell?
JOCASTA. He comes from Corinth, and he brings thee word
    That Polybus, thy father, lives no more.
OEDIPUS. What say'st thou, friend? Tell me thy tale thyself.
MESSENGER. If I must needs report the story clear,

Know well that he has gone the way of death.   990
OEDIPUS. Was it by plot, or chance of natural death?
MESSENGER. An old man's frame a little stroke lays low!
OEDIPUS. He suffered, then, it seems, from some disease?
MESSENGER. E'en so, and many a weary month he passed.
OEDIPUS. Ha! ha! Why now, my queen, should we regard
    The Pythian hearth oracular, or birds
    In mid-air crying?[20] By their auguries,
    I was to slay my father. And he dies,
    And the grave hides him; and I find myself
    Handling no sword; unless for love of me   1000
    He pined away, and so I caused his death.
    So Polybus is gone, and with him lie,
    In Hades whelmed, those worthless oracles.
JOCASTA. Did I not tell thee this long time ago?
OEDIPUS. Thou didst, but I was led away by fears.
JOCASTA. Dismiss them, then, for ever from thy thoughts!
OEDIPUS. And yet that "incest"; must I not fear that?
JOCASTA. Why should we fear, when chance rules everything,
    And foresight of the future there is none;
    'Tis best to live at random, as one can.   1010
    But thou, fear not that marriage with thy mother:
    Such things men oft have dreams of; but who cares
    The least about them lives the happiest.
OEDIPUS. Right well thou speakest all things, save that she
    Still lives that bore me, and I can but fear,
    Seeing that she lives, although thou speakest well.
JOCASTA. And yet thy father's grave's a spot of light.
OEDIPUS. 'Tis so: yet while she liveth there is fear.
MESSENGER. Who is this woman about whom ye fear?
OEDIPUS. 'Tis Merope, old sir, who lived with Polybus.   1020
MESSENGER. And what leads you to think of her with fear?
OEDIPUS. A fearful oracle, my friend, from God.
MESSENGER. Canst tell it; or must others ask in vain?
OEDIPUS. Most readily; for Loxias said of old
    The doom of incest lay on me, and I
    With mine own hands should spill my father's blood.
    And therefore Corinth long ago I left,
    And journeyed far, right prosperously I own;—
    And yet 'tis sweet to see a parent's face.
MESSENGER. And did this fear thy steps to exile lead?   1030
OEDIPUS. I did not wish to take my father's life.

---

[20] The "Pythian hearth," with special reference to the apparent failure of the Delphic oracle; "birds," to that of the auguries of Teiresias.

MESSENGER. Why, the, O king, did I who came with good
    Not free thee from this fear that haunts thy soul?
OEDIPUS. For this, I own, I owe thee worthy thanks.
MESSENGER. For this, I own, I chiefly came to thee;
    That I on thy return may prosper well.
OEDIPUS. But I return not while a parent lives.
MESSENGER. 'Tis clear, my son, thou know'st not what thou dost.
OEDIPUS. What is't? By all the Gods, old man, speak out.
MESSENGER. If 'tis for them thou fearest to return...   1040
OEDIPUS. I fear lest Phœbus prove himself too true.
MESSENGER. Is it lest thou shouldst stain thy soul through them?
OEDIPUS. This selfsame fear, old man, for ever haunts me.
MESSENGER. And know'st thou not there is no cause for fear?
OEDIPUS. Is there no cause if I was born their son?
MESSENGER. None is there. Polybus is naught to thee.
OEDIPUS. What say'st thou? Did not Polybus beget me?
MESSENGER. No more than he thou speak'st to; just as much.
OEDIPUS. How could a father's claim become as naught?
MESSENGER. Well, neither he begat thee nor did I.   1050
OEDIPUS. Why, then, did he acknowledge me as his?
MESSENGER. He at my hands received thee as a gift.
OEDIPUS. And could he love another's child so much?
MESSENGER. Yes; for this former childlessness wrought on him.
OEDIPUS. And gav'st thou me as buying or as finding?
MESSENGER. I found thee in Kithæron's shrub-grown hollow.
OEDIPUS. And for what cause didst travel thitherwards?
MESSENGER. I had the charge to tend the mountain flocks.
OEDIPUS. Was thou a shepherd born, or seeking hire?
MESSENGER. At any rate, my son, I saved thee then.   1060
OEDIPUS. What evil, plight, then, didst thou find me in?
MESSENGER. The sinews of thy feet would tell that tale.
OEDIPUS. Ah, me! why speak'st thou of that ancient wrong?
MESSENGER. I freed thee when thy insteps both were pierced.
OEDIPUS. A foul disgrace I had in swaddling clothes.
MESSENGER. Thus from his chance there came the name thou
    bearest.
OEDIPUS. [*Starting*] Who gave the name, my father or my mother;
    In heaven's name tell me?
MESSENGER. This I do not know;
    Who gave thee to me better knows than I.   1070
OEDIPUS. Didst thou, then, take me from another's hand,
    Not finding me thyself?
MESSENGER. Not I, indeed;
    Another shepherd made a gift of thee.
OEDIPUS. Who was he? know'st thou where to find him out?

MESSENGER. They called him one of those that Laius owned.
OEDIPUS. Mean's thou the former sovereign of this land?
MESSENGER. E'en so. He fed the flocks of him thou nam'st.
OEDIPUS. And is he living still that I might see him?
MESSENGER. You, his own countrymen, should know that
    best.   1080
OEDIPUS. Is there of you who stand and listen here
    One who has known the shepherd that he tells of,
    Or seeing him upon the hills or here?
    If so, declare it; 'tis full time to speak!
CHORUS. I think that this is he whom from the hills
    But now thou soughtest. But Jocasta here
    Could tell thee this with surer word than I.
OEDIPUS. Knowest thou, my queen, the man whom late we sent
    To fetch; and him of whom this stranger speaks?
JOCASTA. [*With forced calmness*] Whom did he speak of?   1090
    Care not thou for it,
    But wish his words may be but idle tales.
OEDIPUS. I cannot fail, once getting on the scent,
    To track at last the secret of my birth.
JOCASTA. Ah, by the Gods, if that thou valuest life
    Inquire no further. Let my woe suffice.
OEDIPUS. Take heart; though I should turn out thrice a slave,
    Born of a thrice vile mother, thou art still
    Free from all stain.
JOCASTA. Yet, I implore thee, pause!   1100
    Yield to my counsels, do not do this deed.
OEDIPUS. I may not yield, and fail to search it out.
JOCASTA. And yet good counsels give I, for thy good.
OEDIPUS. This "for my good" has been my life's long plague.
JOCASTA. Who thou art, hapless, mayst thou never know!
OEDIPUS. Will some one bring that shepherd to me here?
    Leave her to glory in her high descent.
JOCASTA. Woe! woe! ill-fated one! my last word this,
    This only, and no more for evermore. [*Rushes out.*]
CHORUS. Why has thy queen, O Oedipus, gone forth   1110
    In her wild sorrow rushing. Much I fear
    Lest from such silence evil deeds burst out.
OEDIPUS. Burst out what will, I seek to know my birth,
    Low though it be, and she perhaps is shamed
    (For, like a woman, she is proud of heart)
    At thoughts of my low birth; but I, who count
    Myself the child of Fortune, fear no shame.
    My mother she, and she has prospered me.
    And so the months that span my life have made me

Both high and low; but whatsoe'er I be,   1120
Such as I am I am, and needs must on
To fathom all the secret of my birth.

STROPH

CHORUS. If the seer's gift be mine,
        Or skill in counsel wise,
Thou, O Kithæron, when the morrow comes,
        Our full-moon festival,
Shalt fail not to resound
        The voice that greets thee, fellow-citizen,
        Parent and nurse of Oedipus;
And we will on thee weave our choral dance,   1130
As bringing to our princes glad good news.
Hail, hail! O Phœbus, smile on this our prayer.

ANTISTROPH

Who was it, child, that bore thee?[21]
Blest daughter of the ever-living Ones,
Or meeting in the ties of love with Pan,
        Who wanders o'er the hills,
        Or with thee, Loxias, for to thee are dear
All the high lawns where roam the pasturing flocks;
Or was it he who rules Kyllene's height;
        Or did the Bacchic God,   1140
        Upon the mountain's peak,
Receive thee as the gift of some fair nymph
        Of Helicon's fair band,
With whom he sports and wantons evermore?

OEDIPUS. If I must needs conjecture, who as yet
        Ne'er met the man, I think I see the shepherd,
        Whom this long while we sought for. With the years
        His age fits well. And now I see, besides,
        My servants bring him. Thou perchance canst say
        From former knowledge yet more certainly.   1150
CHORUS. I know him well, O king! For this man stood,
        If any, known as Laius' faithful slave.

---

[21] The Chorus, thinking only of the wonder of Oedipus's birth, plays with the conjecture that he is the offspring of the Gods, of Pan, the God of the hills, or Apollo, the prophet God, or Hermes, worshipped on Kyllene in Arcadia; or Bacchos, roaming on the highest peaks of Parnassos. The Heliconian nymphs are, of course, the Muses.

[*Enter* SHEPHERD]

OEDIPUS. Thee first I ask, Corinthian stranger, say,
    Is this the man?
MESSENGER. The very man thou seek'st.
OEDIPUS. Ho, there, old man. Come hither, look on me,
    And tell me all. Did Laius own thee once?
SHEPHERD. Not as a slave from market, but home-reared.
OEDIPUS. What was thy work, or what thy mode of life?
SHEPHERD. Near all my life I followed with the flock.   1160
OEDIPUS. And in what regions didst thou chiefly dwell?
SHEPHERD. Now 'twas Kithæron, now on neighbouring fields.
OEDIPUS. Know'st thou this man? Didst ever see him there?
SHEPHERD. What did he do? Of what man speakest thou?
OEDIPUS. This man now present. Did ye ever meet?
SHEPHERD. My memory fails when taxed thus suddenly.
MESSENGER. No wonder that, my lord. But I'll remind him
    Right well of things forgotten. Well I know
    He'll call to mind when on Kithæron's fields,
    He with a double flock, and I with one,   1170
    I was his neighbour during three half years,
    From springtide on to autumn; and in winter
    I drove my flocks to mine own fold, and he
    To those of Laius. [*To* SHEPHERD] Is this false or true?
SHEPHERD. Thou tell'st the truth, although long years have passed.
MESSENGER. Come, then, say, on. Rememberest thou a boy
    Thou gav'st me once, that I might rear him up
    As mine own child?
SHEPHERD. Why askest thou of this?
MESSENGER. Here stands he, fellow! that same tiny boy!   1180
SHEPHERD. A curse befall thee! Wilt not hold thy tongue?
OEDIPUS. Rebuke him not, old man; thy words need more
    The language of reproaches than do his.
SHEPHERD. Say, good my lord, what fault have I committed?
OEDIPUS. This, that thou tell'st not of the child he asks for.
SHEPHERD. Yes, for he speaks in blindness, wasting breath.
OEDIPUS. Thou wilt not speak for favour, but a blow… [*Strikes him.*]
SHEPHERD. By all the Gods, hurt not my feeble age.
OEDIPUS. Will no one bind his hands behind his back?[22]
SHEPHERD. O man most wretched! what, then, wilt thou
    learn?   1190
OEDIPUS. Gav'st thou this man the boy of whom he asks?
SHEPHERD. I gave him. Would that day had been my last!

---

[22] *Sc.,* Will no one scourge him at my command, and make him confess?

OEDIPUS. That doom will soon be thine if thou speak'st wrong.
SHEPHERD. Nay, much more shall I perish if I speak.
OEDIPUS. This fellow, as it seems, would tire us out.
SHEPHERD. Not so. I said long since I gave it him.
OEDIPUS. Whence came it? Was the child thine own or not?
SHEPHERD. Mine own 'twas not, but some one gave it me,
OEDIPUS. Which of our people, or beneath what roof?
SHEPHERD. Oh, by the Gods, my master, ask no more!   1200
OEDIPUS. Thou diest if I question this again.
SHEPHERD. Some one it was in Laius' household born.
OEDIPUS. Was it a slave, or some one born to him?
SHEPHERD. Ah, me! I stand upon the very brink
    Where most I dread to speak.
OEDIPUS. And I to hear:
    And yet I needs must hear it, come what may.
SHEPHERD. The boy was said to be his son; but she,
    Thy queen within, could tell thee best the truth.
OEDIPUS. What! was it she who gave it?   1210
SHEPHERD. Yea, O king!
OEDIPUS. And to what end?
SHEPHERD. To make away with it.
OEDIPUS. And dared a mother...?
SHEPHERD. Evil doom she feared.
OEDIPUS. What doom?
SHEPHERD. 'Twas said that he his sire should kill.
OEDIPUS. Why, then, didst thou to this old man resign him?
SHEPHERD. I pitied him, O master, and I thought
    That he would bear him to another land,   1220
    Whence he himself had come. But him he saved
    For direst evil. For if thou be he
    Whom this man speaks of, thou art born to ill.
OEDIPUS. Woe! woe! woe! woe! all cometh clear at last.
    O light, may I ne'er look on thee again,
    Who now am seen owing my birth to those
    To whom I ought not, and with whom I ought not
    In wedlock living, whom I ought not slaying. [*Exit.*]

STROPHE I

CHORUS. Ah, race of mortal men,
    How as a thing of naught   1230
    I count ye, though ye live;
    For who is there of men
    That more of blessing knows
    Than just a little while

In a vain show to stand,
And, having stood, to fall?
With thee before mine eyes,
Thy destiny, e'en thine,
Ill-fated Oedipus,
I can count no man blest.   1240

ANTISTROPHE I

For thou, with wondrous skill,
Taking thine aim, didst hit
Success, in all things prosperous;
And didst, O Zeus! destroy
The Virgin with her talons bent,
And sayings wild and dark;
And against many deaths
A tower and strong defence
Didst for my country rise;
And therefore dost thou bear the name of king,   1250
With highest glory crowned,
Ruling in mighty Thebes.

STROPHE II

And now, who lives than thou more miserable?
Who equals thee in wild woes manifold,
In shifting turns of life?
Ah, noble one, our Oedipus!
For whom the selfsame port
Sufficed for sire and son,
In wedlock's haven met:
Ah how, ah how, thou wretched one, so long   1260
Could that incestuous bed
Receive thee, and be dumb?

ANTISTROPHE II

Time, who sees all things, he hath found thee out,
Against thy will, and long ago condemned
The wedlock none may wed,
Begetter and begotten
In strange confusion joined.
Ah, child of Laius! ah!
Would that I ne'er had looked upon thy face!
For I mourn sore exceedingly,   1270

From lips with wailing full.
In simplest truth, by thee I rose from death,
By thee I close mine eyes in deadly sleep.

[*Enter* SECOND MESSENGER]

SEC. MESSENGER. Ye chieftains, honoured most in this our land,
    For all the deeds ye hear of, all ye see,
    How great a wailing will ye raise, if still
    Ye truly love the house of Labdacus;
    For sure I think that neither Ister's stream
    Nor Phasis' floods could purify this house,[23]
    Such horrors does it hold. But all too soon,   1280
    Will we or will we not, they'll come to light.
    Self-chosen sorrows ever pain men most.
CHORUS. The ills we knew before lacked nothing meet
    For plaint and moaning. Now, what add'st thou more?
SEC. MESSENGER. Quickest for me to speak, and thee to learn;
    Our godlike queen Jocasta—she is dead.
CHORUS. Ah, crushed with many sorrows! How and why?
SEC. MESSENGER. Herself she slew. The worst of all that passed
    I must pass o'er, for none were there to see.
    Yet, far as memory suffers me to speak,   1290
    That sorrow-stricken woman's end I'll tell;
    How, yielding to her passion, on she passed
    Within the porch, made straightway for the couch,
    Her bridal bed, with both hands tore her hair,
    And as she entered, dashing through the doors,
    Calls on her Laius, dead long years ago,
    Remembering all that birth of long ago,
    Which brought him death, and left to her who bore,
    With his own son a hateful motherhood.
    And o'er her bed she wailed, where she had borne   1300
    Spouse to her spouse, and children to her child;
    And how she perished after this I know not;
    For Oedipus struck in with woeful cry,
    And we no longer looked upon her fate,
    But gazed on him as to and fro he rushed,
    For so he comes, and asks us for a sword,
    Wherewith to smite the wife that wife was none,
    The bosom stained by those accursed births,
    Himself, his children—so, as thus he raves,
    Some spirit shows her to him (none of us   1310

---

[23] Istros as the great river of Europe, Phasis of Asia.

Who stood hard by had done so): with a shout
Most terrible, as some one led him on,
Through the two gates he leapt, and from the hasp
He slid the hollow bolt, and falls within;
And there we saw his wife had hung herself,
By twisted cords suspended. When her form
He saw, poor wretch! with one wild, fearful cry,
The twisted rope he loosens, and she fell,
Ill-starred one, on the ground. Then came a sight
Most fearful. Tearing from her robe the clasps,   1320
All chased with gold, with which she decked herself,
He with them struck the pupils of his eyes,
Such words as these exclaiming: "They should see
No more the ills he suffered or had done;
But in the dark should look, in time to come,
On those they ought not, not know whom they would."
With such like wails, not once or twice alone,
Raising the lids, he tore his eyes, and they,
All bleeding, stained his cheek, nor ceased to pour
Thick clots of gore, but still the purple shower   1330
Fell fast and full, a very rain of blood.
Such were the ills that fell on both of them,
Not on one only, wife and husband both.
His former fortune, which he held of old,
Was rightly honoured; but for this day's doom
Wailing and woe, and death and shame, all forms
That man can name of evil, none have failed.
CHORUS. And hath the wretched man a pause of ill?
SEC. MESSENGER. He calls to us to ope the gates, and show
To all in Thebes his father's murderer,   1340
His mother's... Foul and fearful were the words
He spoke. I dare not speak them. Then he said
That he would cast himself adrift, nor stay
At home accursèd, as himself had cursed.
Some stay he surely needs, or guiding hand,
For greater is the ill than he can bear,
And this he soon will show thee, for the bolts
Of the two gates are opening, and thou'lt see
A sight to touch e'en hatred's self with pity.

[*The doors of the Palace are thrown open, and* OEDIPUS *is seen
    within.*]

CHORUS. Oh, fearful, piteous sight! 1350
  Most fearful of all woes
   I hitherto have known! What madness strange
  Has come on thee, thou wretched one?
  What power with one fell swoop,
  Ills heaping upon ills,
  Each greater than the last,
  Has marked thee for its prey?
  Woe! woe! thou doomed one, wishing much to ask,
  And much to learn, and much to gaze into,
   I cannot look on thee, 1360
   So horrible the sight!
OEDIPUS. Ah, woe! ah, woe! ah, woe!
  Woe for my misery!
  Where am I wand'ring in my utter woe?
  Where floats my voice in air?
  Dread power, where leadest thou?
CHORUS. To doom of dread nor sight nor speech may bear.
OEDIPUS. O cloud of darkest guilt
  That onwards sweeps with dread ineffable,
  Resistless, borne along by evil blast, 1370
   Woe, woe, and woe again!
  How through my soul there darts the sting of pain,
  The memory of my crimes.
CHORUS. And who can wonder that in such dire woes
  Thou mournest doubly, bearing twofold ills?
OEDIPUS. Ah, friend,
  Thou only keepest by me, faithful found,
  Nor dost the blind one slight.
   Woe, woe,
  For thou escap'st me not, I know thee well; 1380
  Though all is dark, I still can hear thy voice.
CHORUS. O man of fearful deeds, how couldst thou bear
  Thine eyes to outrage? What power stirred thee to it?
OEDIPUS. Apollo! oh, my friends, the God, Apollo!
  Who worketh all my woes—yes, all my woes.
  No human hand but mine has done this deed.
   What need for me to see,
  When nothing's left that's sweet to look upon?
CHORUS. Too truly dost thou speak the thing that is.
OEDIPUS. Yea, what remains to see, 1390
   Or what to love, or hear,
   With any touch of joy?
  Lead me away, my friends, with utmost speed,

Lead me away, the foul polluted one,
  Of all men most accursed,
  Most hateful to the Gods.
CHORUS. Ah, wretched one, alike in soul and doom,
  Would that my eyes had never known thy face!
OEDIPUS. Ill fate be his who loosed the fetters sharp,
    That ate into my flesh,   1400
  And freed me from the doom of death,
  And saved me—thankless boon!
  Ah! had I died but then,
  Nor to my friends nor me had been such woe.
CHORUS. That I, too, vainly wish!
OEDIPUS. Yes; then I had not been
    My father's murderer:
  Nor had men pointed to me as the man
  Wedded with her who bore him.
  But now all god-deserted, born in sins,   1410
  In incest joined with her who gave me birth;
  Yea, if there be an evil worse than all,
  It falls on Oedipus!
CHORUS. I may not call thy acts or counsels good,
  For better wert thou dead than living blind.
OEDIPUS. Persuade me not, nor counsel give to show
  That what I did was not the best to do.
  I know not how, on entering Hades dark,
  To look for my own father or my mother,
  Crimes worse than deadly done against them both.   1420
  And though my children's face was sweet to see
  With their growth growing, yet these eyes no more
  That sight shall see, nor citadel, nor tower,
  Nor sacred shrines of Gods whence I, who stood
  Most honoured one in Thebes, myself have banished,
  Commanding all to thrust the godless forth,
  Him whom the Gods do show accursed, the stock
  Of Laius old. And could I dare to look,
  Such dire pollution fixing on myself,
  And meet them face to face? Not so, not so.   1430
  Yea, if I could but stop the stream of sound,
  And dam mine ears against it, I would do it,
  Closing each wretched sense that I might live
  Both blind, and hearing nothing, Sweet 'twould be
  To keep the soul beyond the reach of ills.
  Why, O Kithæron, didst thou shelter me,
  Nor kill me out of hand? I had not shown,
  In that case, all men whence I drew my birth.

O Polybus, and Corinth, and the home
I thought was mine, how strange a growth ye reared,   1440
All fair outside, all rotten at the core;
For vile I stand, descended from the vile.
Ye threefold roads and thickets half concealed,
The hedge, the narrow pass where three ways meet,
Which at my hands did drink my father's blood,
Remember ye what deeds I did in you;
What, hither come, I did?—the marriage rites
That gave me birth, and then, commingling all,
In horrible confusion, showed in one
A father, brother, son, all kindreds mixed,   1450
Mother, and wife, and daughter, hateful names,
All foulest deeds that men have ever done.
But, since, where deeds are evil, speech is wrong,
With utmost speed, by all the Gods, or hide,
Or take my life, or cast me in the sea,
Where nevermore your eyes may look on me.
Come, scorn ye not to touch my misery,
But hearken; fear ye not; no soul but I
Can bear the burden of my countless ills.[24]
CHORUS. The man for what thou need'st is come in time,   1460
Creon, to counsel and to act, for now
He in thy place is left our only guide.[25]
OEDIPUS. Ah, me! what language shall I hold to him,
What trust at his hands claim? In all the past
I showed myself to him most vile and base.

[*Enter* CREON]

CREON. I have not come, O Oedipus, to scorn,
Nor to reproach thee for thy former crimes;
But ye, if ye have lost your sense of shame
For mortal men, yet reverence the light
Of him, our King, the Sun-God, source of life,   1470
Nor sight so foul expose unveiled to view,
Which neither earth, nor shower from heaven nor light,
Can see and welcome. But with utmost speed
Convey him in; for nearest kin alone
Can meetly see and hear their kindred's ills.
OEDIPUS. Oh, by the Gods! since thou, beyond my hopes,

---

[24] I follow Schneidewin in transferring the last lines from Creon (after 1430) to Oedipus.

[25] The two sons of Oedipus, Polyneikes and Eteocles, the Chorus thinks of as too young to reign.

Dost come all noble unto me all base,
In one thing hearken. For thy good I ask.
CREON. And what request seek'st thou so wistfully?
OEDIPUS. Cast me with all thy speed from out this land,   1480
Where nevermore a man may look on me!
CREON. Be sure I would have done so, but I wished
To learn what now the God will bid us do.
OEDIPUS. The oracle was surely clear enough
That I, the parricide, the pest, should die.
CREON. So ran the words. But in our present need
'Tis better to learn surely what to do.
OEDIPUS. And will ye ask for one so vile as I?
CREON. Yea, now thou, too, wouldst trust the voice of God.
OEDIPUS. And this I charge thee, yea, and supplicate,   1490
For her within, provide what tomb thou wilt,
For for thine own most meetly thou wilt care;
But never let this city of my fathers
Be sentenced to receive me as its guest;
But suffer me on yon lone hills to dwell,
Where stands Kithæron, chosen as my tomb
While still I lived, by mother and by sire,
That I may die by those who sought to kill.
And yet this much I know, that no disease,
Nor aught else could have killed me; ne'er from death   1500
Had I been saved but for this destined doom.
But for our fate, whatever comes may come:
And for my boys, O Creon, lay no charge
Of them upon me. They are grown, nor need,
Where'er they be, feel lack of means to live.
But for my two poor girls, all desolate,
To whom their table never brought a meal
Without my presence, but whate'er I touched
They still partook of with me; these I care for.
Yea, let me touch them with my hands, and weep   1510
To them my sorrows. Grant it, O my prince,
        O born of noble nature!
Could I but touch them with my hands, I feel
Still I should have them mine, as when I saw.

[*Enter* ANTIGONE *and* ISMENE]

What say I? What is this?
Do I not hear, ye Gods, their dear, loved tones,
Broken with sobs, and Creon, pitying me,
Hath sent the dearest of my children to me?

Is it not so?
CREON. It is so. I am he who gives thee this,   1520
    Knowing the joy thou hadst in them of old.
OEDIPUS. Good luck have thou! And may the powers on high
    Guard thy path better than they guarded mine!
    Where are ye, O my children? Come, oh, come
    To these your brother's hands, which but now tore
    Your father's eyes, that once were bright to see,
    Who, O my children, blind and knowing naught,
    Became your father—how, I may not tell.
    I weep for you, though sight is mine no more,
    Picturing in mind the sad and dreary life   1530
    Which waits you in the world in years to come;
    For to what friendly gatherings will ye go,
    Or festive joys, from whence, for stately show
    Once yours, ye shall not home return in tears?
    And when ye come to marriageable age,
    Who is there, O my children, rash enough
    To make his own the shame that then will fall
    On those who bore me, and on you as well?
    What evil fails us here? Your father killed
    His father, and was wed in incest foul   1540
    With her who bore him, and ye owe your birth
    To her who gave him his. Such shame as this
    Will men lay on you, and who then will dare
    To make you his in marriage? None, not one,
    My children! but ye needs must waste away,
    Unwedded, childless, Thou, Menœkeus' son,
    Since thou alone art left a father to them
    (For we, their parents, perish utterly),
    Suffer them not to wander husbandless,
    Nor let thy kindred beg their daily bread;   1550
    But look on them with pity, seeing them
    At their age, but for thee, deprived of all.
    O noble soul, I pray thee, touch my hand
    In token of consent. And ye, my girls,
    Had ye the minds to hearken I would fain
    Give ye much counsel. As it is, pray for me
    To live where'er is meet; and for yourselves
    A brighter life than his ye call your sire.
CREON. Enough of tears and words. Go thou within.
OEDIPUS. I needs must yield, however, hard it be.   1560
CREON. In their right season all things prospect best.
OEDIPUS. Know'st thou my wish?
CREON. Speak and I then shall hear.

OEDIPUS. That thou shouldst send me far away from home.
CREON. Thou askest what the Gods alone can give.
OEDIPUS. And yet I go most hated of the Gods.
CREON. And therefore it may chance thou gain'st thy wish.
OEDIPUS. And dost thou promise, then, to grant it me?
CREON. I am not wont to utter idle words.
OEDIPUS. Lead me, then, hence.   1570
CREON. Go thou, but leave the girls.
OEDIPUS. Ah, take them not from me!
CREON. Thou must not think
  To have thy way in all things all thy life.
  Thou hadst it once, yet went it ill with thee.
CHORUS. Ye men of Thebes, behold this Oedipus,
  Who knew the famous riddle and was noblest,
  Who envied no one's fortune and success.
  And, lo,! in what a sea of direst woe
  He now is plunged. From hence the lesson draw,   1580
  To reckon no man happy till ye see
  The closing day; until he pass the bourn
  Which severs life from death, unscathed by woe.

THE END

Made in the USA
San Bernardino, CA
04 November 2019